FROM THE FOUNDER OF THE INSECURITY PROJECT

THE
SELF-PERMISSION
METHOD

How to succeed at life without using self-discipline.

JAEMIN FRAZER

THE SELF-PERMISSION METHOD. HOW TO SUCCEED AT LIFE WITHOUT USING SELF-DISCIPLINE.

2024 © by Jaemin Frazer.
All rights reserved. Printed in Australia.

No part of this book may be used or reproduced in any manner whatsoever without written permission except in the case of brief quotation embodied in critical articles and reviews.

For information contact the author at www.jaeminfrazer.com

National Library of Australia Cataloguing-in-Publication entry:
Frazer, Jaemin, author.
The Self Permission Method. How to succeed at life without self-discipline / Jaemin Frazer.
ISBN: 978-0-6488942-5-4 (paperback)
Self Help
Mind Body

Other books by Jaemin:

1. Unhindered – The Seven Essential Practices for Overcoming Insecurity,

2. Elegantly Simple Solutions to Complex People Problems,

3. Leverage – How to change the people you love for all the right reasons and get the relationships you deserve, and

4. The One Minute Coach – 365 Thought provoking insights to start your day.

Contents

Introduction	1
1. Self-discipline is overrated	5
2. The great misunderstanding	21
3. Self-permission	29
4. The Four Safety Concerns	37
5. Safety concern number one	
– You don't trust yourself	39
6. How to rebuild trust	91
7. Safety concern number two	
– You keep showing up needy	120
8. Fully becoming an adult	143
9. Safety concern number three	
– Your gameplay sucks	153
10. Safety concern number four	
– An incongruent avatar	187
11. Permission granted	199
12. The Pressure Test	203
Conclusion	221

Introduction

Stuart called me in a flap. He was frustrated, upset, and embarrassed.

Stuart ran a very successful, multi-million-dollar company with his business partner, but of late his partner had been left carrying the business because Stuart was in such a weird space within himself. He explained that he was missing deadlines for content creation, procrastinating about important tasks that were his responsibility to complete, and having to drag his sorry ass out of bed each morning with a sense of dread about what the day had in store.

When he called me, he explained that it was like someone had pulled a bunch of fuses out in his internal motivation switch board and nothing was working properly.

This was more terrifying to him because he'd always been such a high achiever. His business partner seemed ok to pick up the slack for now, but that's only because he'd defended off the sudden performance drop off as a minor glitch and promised to be back on track shortly.

Yet Stuart had enough self-awareness to know that this was no minor glitch. He was in real trouble. This issue had gone on long enough for him to realise it was not going to magically fix itself.

He'd been aware of my work on insecurity before, but always dismissed it as irrelevant because of how successful he was and how confident that success made him feel.

He confessed that often when he heard me banging on about the danger of unresolved insecurity, his internal dialogue was some version of: "F*ck off…I'm not insecure! Look at all the excellent things I'm doing."

Yet, when all his usual go-to motivation hacks to get himself back in the game had repeatedly failed, and all the excellent things had dried up, it was my name that kept popping into his awareness.

"I've got no f*cking idea what is wrong with me Jaemin, but I woke up this morning with you on my mind, and I get the sense that you may know exactly what's happening," he told me.

I acknowledged his suffering and then agreed with his

Introduction

conclusion. "Yeah…of course," I said. "There's nothing mysterious about this at all. You are right in the heart of the mid-life pinch point. You are totally correct. Someone has disconnected your fuses and is deliberately sabotaging your success right now. The good news is, I can tell you exactly who it was, why they did it, and most importantly, how to get them all plugged back in again."

This book is the complete explanation of how Stuart, or anyone, can get the fuses put back in and access true and lasting motivation, performance, and play. It is for anyone who has watched themselves achieve high level results in the past with significant levels of motivation, commitment, and drive, but now feels so frustrated with their inability to continue performing at the same level.

If you are willing to see that the high-performance results of your younger years were achieved by using your best energy AGAINST yourself, you may then anticipate that it is possible to achieve even more when you stop fighting your way forward and discover how to use your best energy WITH yourself instead.

This is a movement away from harsh, critical, abusive self-discipline as the main source of human motivation and is the next frontier in the evolution of the human consciousness. The thinking that has once been the high-water mark and seen as best practice for ambitious humans to get the best out of themselves is now out of date and in need of a radical overhaul.

Without a road map for ambitious mid-lifers to access the next season of motivation, they will flounder, fail, and suffer. And the world will be robbed of their contribution and true essence.

This is the way forward. Self-permission supersedes self-discipline. It is the update, the upgrade, and the far superior form of motivation.

If you'd like to continue down the self-discipline road spurred on by a host of ultra-masculine, ex-military hard-arses like Jocko Willink, David Goggins, or Ant Middleton you are welcome to continue the abusive relationship with yourself, but if you are exhausted and bewildered enough by their approach and ready for an upgrade, you're about to discover something far better and far more beautiful.

In the pages of this short book, is a new and better way, and a clear upgrade in the way you seek to access motivation, peak performance, and success. Central to this process, you will also discover how to clean the space within your relationship with yourself and become a genuinely good human in the process.

1.
Self-discipline is overrated

Before explaining how self-permission works and specifically the conditions that must be fulfilled to have it granted to you, allow me to explain why self-discipline is not the answer to Stuart's problem even though gurus, authors and experts would have you believe it is still the only way to improve your results.

Self-regulation theory

Let's start by examining the academic research on the science of will-power.

Most of the trouble with self-discipline can be credited back to the single source of the self-regulation theory developed by Roy Baumeister.

Self-regulation theory (SRT) is a system of conscious

personal management that involves the process of guiding one's own thoughts, behaviours, and feelings to reach goals. [1]

Baumeister is also credited with the model for self-control. It was he who first introduced the concept of ego depletion, a term used to describe the idea that self-control depended on a limited source of energy. Baumeister suggested that self-control deteriorates over time and likened willpower to muscles that get tired. He concluded that willpower is a limited resource and so we all have limited capacity for self-regulation.

Although this model has largely been discredited, it still forms the basis for how most people feel about the subject of motivation. The idea of ego depletion is still accepted as true in popular psychology.

Based on this finding, his research then moved into addressing what can be done to strengthen this muscle and increase our motivation to do the right thing and the ability to manage undesirable behaviour. Baumeister and co devoted much time and energy to the science of using energy against yourself to fix this problem of ego depletion.

---

1 https://en.wikipedia.org/wiki/Self-regulation_theory#:~:text=The%20four%20components%20of%20self,internal%20strength%20to%20control%20urges.

1. Self-discipline is overrated

While their observation that willpower wanes over time is accurate, the lack of curiosity about *why* this is true is a major oversite. Assuming this is simply a human flaw to be managed, without questioning why this could in fact be a natural, normal, healthy, and intentional part of the entire system of human motivation, has led to the tragedy of self-discipline becoming the accepted panacea.

Flowing on from the research on this idea, the best advice that comes from this model is an example of just how vacuous this kind of academic theory really is:

> *"We noted that success at building self-control through exercises has been inconsistent, so it is also necessary to explore why some regimens work better than others. Finding a reliable way to improve self-control would not only shed light on how the self functions but would also have practical value for therapists, coaches, educators, parents, and many others."*[2]

So here we have the leading thinker on the subject of regulating your own behaviour saying that there is no evidence to say you can genuinely get better at this!

Knowing this doesn't help anyone have better self-control, it just makes people more likely to concede that they are

---

2   http://assets.csom.umn.edu/assets/166733.pdf

'only human', and as such, will always struggle to control the parts of themselves they don't like or understand.

Baumeister observed that self-discipline is limited, and exercises to build will power muscle don't work consistently. Surely that would lead to one high quality question. All other muscles respond consistently to strength building exercise, so if willpower is also a muscle why could it not be strengthened as well?

The only logic is that there must be some internal resistance working against the strengthening of the willpower greater than the willpower itself.

Why would the most loving and wise parts of you help you create low quality, self-destructive, short-sighted and maddening strategy all built on a horrible misunderstanding and personal betrayal?

In the mid-life season. The harder you try and build the muscle, the harder the internal handbrake comes on to stop you.

1. Self-discipline is overrated

Stay hard

Following on from this academic misdirection, David Goggins takes the faulty self-control concept and puts it on steroids. His two books – *Can't Hurt Me* and *Never Finished* are brutal descriptions of his hellish obsession with Baumeister's self-control theory.

When it comes to pushing the physical limits of the human body and mind, without question, he is the elite of the elite. He is the only member of the US armed forces to complete Navy SEAL Training, the U.S Army Ranger School and Air Force Tactical Air Controller Training. He has competed in multiple ultra-marathons and ultra-triathlons. He is considered one of the world's greatest endurance athletes and has proved on numerous occasions that his ability to torture himself in the pursuit of being better than anyone else is superhuman.

Goggins' approach to motivation is to be aggressively badass towards yourself. Here is a summary of his teachings:

> *Find the things you hate and force yourself to do them again and again until you are numb to the suffering. And then do more. Always do more than the next guy. Keep doing more than you can, for longer than you can,*

tolerating more pain than you can handle. Suppress and ignore pain until you can't hear it anymore. Callous your mind. Push hardest when you want to quit the most. Your work is NEVER finished.

His message to his followers is that someone is always coming for you. Someone is always trying to better you.

*Every time you look over your shoulder some motherf*cker (His words) is trying to take your title. You can never relax. You must stay hard until the very end.*[3]

The main problem with Goggins' approach to midlife motivation is there is no end in sight. You've got to fight against time, the world, the next guy, pain, and most importantly yourself. There is no rest.

It all sounds a bit exhausting.

The source of motivation is always energy **against.** To stay hard, he must have an adversary to beat. Obviously, this is a very powerful motivator and countless individuals have found extraordinary power by using this approach – but at what cost?

---

[3] From his book "You can't hurt me – Master your mind and defy the odds", Lioncrest, 2018.

1. Self-discipline is overrated

The worst part of this strategy is that in the absence of real conflict, you must invent some. If you can only get yourself motivated in the presence of an adversary, then you must make stuff up and torture yourself with inflated and imagined attacks against you.

The world becomes your foe.

You turn friends into enemies.

And you must treat yourself like an enemy too.

Is everyone and everything really out to get you? What if no one really cares about how many pull ups you can do, how far you can run or how much pain you can endure? What if the 'inner bitch', is actually a beautiful, kind and loving part of you that is consistently misunderstand and mistreated?

While Goggins has a huge fan base, and many people credit his advice as the main reason they were able to turn their lives around does not exclude his message and methodology from scrutiny.

Yes, this strategy works. You can callous your mind, stay hard, and drive yourself beyond the normal limits of pain. But just because it works, doesn't mean it's a good idea or that there is no collateral damage. And just because it works for now, in no way guarantees it will work in the future. It is brutal and unsustainable at the same time.

Jocko Willink

Jocko Willink, author of *Extreme Ownership*, has a very similar philosophy.

Here is a summary of his motivation strategy:

> *Don't worry about motivation. Motivation is fickle. It comes and goes. It is unreliable and when you are counting on motivation to get your goals accomplished— you will likely fall short. Don't expect to be motivated every day to get out there and make things happen. You won't be. Don't count on motivation. Count on discipline. You must become disciplined to overcome obstacles and develop the best version of yourself whether you want to be stronger, faster, smarter, better, or healthier. Discipline comes from within and must be a conscious decision and sustained every day with no excuses. Discipline keeps people on the right path to success because it allows no excuses for lack of action. You must wake up with the attitude that the 'count is zero' every day meaning you must prove yourself all over again. You have to earn your seat at the table.*

1. Self-discipline is overrated

Even though we've already seen the flaws in Baumeister's self-control model, Willink blindly continues to preach that discipline begets discipline and will propagates more will. He says:

> 'Nurturing discipline is important to maintaining progress over the long-term because it is too easy to fall back into old habits that impede progress.' Don't do what makes you happy. Do what makes you better. Do not let your mind control you, control your mind and then you can set it free.'[4]

Dominate and control

When interviewed on Russel Brand's podcast[5] he said that the best way to deal with negative self-talk is not to have any self-talk at all. Instead, his simple instruction is to shut it down. He explains that there is no internal conversation with himself. He does not listen to any voice in his head for fear of entering a negotiation about the thing he must do. He proudly declares: "I do not negotiate with weakness."

In any other relational context, that is the pure definition of abuse. One party completely dominates, controls,

---

4 From his book "Discipline equals freedom. Field manual" St Martins press, 2020
5 https://www.facebook.com/watch/?v=609015321010067

supresses, and shuts out the other. Suggesting this as the very best way to treat *yourself* is horrific.

Extreme ownership is all about maintaining the illusion of control. The tragedy of Willink's method and message is how desperately he is grappling for control and how completely he imagines he has achieved it.

> *Look at this. I am in control! Look at how powerful and strong I am!*

> *Ok...for now. But let's see how this ends, you monster.*

You cannot control yourself. Self-control is not real. You are simply managing yourself. Just like when someone else manages you, they think they control you, all the while resentment, bitterness, and anger simmer beneath the surface, edging closer to breaking point where they tell you to go stick it up your arse.

It's all smiles and compliance on the surface, and rebellion and rage underneath. If you supress, control, manage, ignore, and shut out another person for long enough, there is only one way the relationship ends.

If you want to win now through abuse, domination, and control, you better get ready to reap what you've sown 10-fold, as soon as the opportunity arises.

1. Self-discipline is overrated

Every single gangster movie ever made ends the same way. The crime boss who rises to the top by the sheer ruthlessness and brutality of his life, is one false move from being eaten alive by the next monster. He who lives by the sword dies by the sword.[6] That is the only way the story ends. Peace gained through violence is only ever momentary.

There is no peace. Your enemies have not been defeated permanently; they are simply biding their time until your arrogance leaves you vulnerable to attack. And then you are mercilessly stripped of all power and humiliated as the fool you really are.

Good soldiers are not good humans

It is worth remembering that both Willink and Goggins come from a military background which is based on the necessity of dehumanising individuals to make them effective soldiers. The differences between good soldiers and good humans are vast. There is no guarantee that good soldiers are good humans at all.

This makes it all the more strange that anyone would think it is a good idea to take advice on how to be human from ex-military heroes like Willink and Goggins in the first place.

---

6   Words of Jesus from Matthew 26:52

The war against Resistance

Steven Pressfield's book *The War of Art,* is widely celebrated as the go-to solution for struggling artists, authors, musicians, and creatives. In fact, author of *The 4 Hour Work Week*, Tim Ferriss, says it is the best book title ever! The main focus of all Pressfield's work is what to do with the internal resistance you face when trying to be creatively productive. He teaches people how to overcome their internal resistance and do the thing that you know you must.

Although Pressfield is indeed a prolific author, he is more celebrated for his theory on the war against art than his art itself. So, whether this is the strategy that has actually worked for him, I'm far from convinced. I count his theory as the most tragic of all the self-discipline experts because he is the oldest which means he's been beating the shit out of himself the longest.

Resistance (with a capital R) is the name he gives to the invisible force inside of us that stops us from doing creative work. Pressfield says the best way to beat the resistance is to personify it as an external force trying to ruin your creative work through trickery and other nefarious means. You then must fight directly against this elusive character called Resistance if you have any chance of bringing your creative work to the world.

1. Self-discipline is overrated

Pressfield says openly that after all these years of being a professional writer he is still afraid of the work, still feels sick to his stomach whenever he sits down to write, and still is at war with the Resistance to do the things he must.

He teaches five keys to winning this war with Resistance:[7]

1. Recognise the resistance – See it as a tricky, mean, enemy that is trying to stop you doing what you must.

2. Expect fear – Fear is a natural part of doing creative work. In fact, the central message of his book is that your creative work will really take off when you accept that it's normal to feel emotions like fear, self-doubt, and 'not wanting to do it.'

3. Work anyway – That is to see yourself as a professional who doesn't have the luxury of only working when they feel like. You've just got to do the work regardless.

4. Love misery – Accept that the path you've chosen is a very difficult one. The life of an artist is filled with adversity and failure.

5. Harness the muse – It is following a routine that invites inspiration into our lives and allows us to harness the personified force that is the source of this inspiration.

---

[7] Summarised from The War of Art – Steven Pressfied. Black Irish Entertainment, 2012

His more recent books, *'Do the Work'* and *'Put Your Ass Where Your Heart Wants to Be'* continues his theme of being creative by fighting against this Resistance.

The tragedy of Pressfield's 'War of Art' message is that it is based on a faulty assumption that if someone or something resists you it MUST be your enemy.

That is a horrible oversimplification which is clearly untrue.

The simplest rebuttal of this logic is to watch a loving parent stop their toddler from running onto the road. Even though the child may not understand why the parent is blocking their path, the parent must resist them anyway otherwise the child is likely to be injured or killed.

In the same way, while it may seem hard to reconcile why part of you would be resisting progress towards your stated goals, what if there is a loving reason that you have not yet understood?

As such, fighting against your own internal resistance is never justified. In fact, as a mature adult, with the capacity for introspection and awareness, it is perhaps one of the most shortsighted, arrogant, and egregious acts of self-betrayal possible.

1. Self-discipline is overrated

If you have gone to war with your resistance, any temporary sense of winning this war is done so at the expense of your own soul. You are fighting yourself in a war that is based on a misunderstanding.

Unlike Pressfied, when I write, I promise you I am not at war with any resistance.

My main message is the complete opposite of his: CEASEFIRE!!! Stop the war. You idiots are on the same bloody team. As soon as you finally realise that both sides of you want the same thing, the war ends. In fact, there is no reason for war at all.

The misplaced energy and enthusiasm against your own wise council ranks amongst other war time tragedies whereby arrogant and conceited generals ordered wave after wave of brave young men into hopeless situations with guaranteed death.

The famous coming together of French, German and Scottish forces on Christmas Eve 1914 to pause hostilities and join in celebrating the birth of Christ, highlights what happens when waring men realise their enemies are in fact their brothers.[8]

---

8   https://en.wikipedia.org/wiki/Christmas_truce

So impacted by this experience of togetherness, whole battalions had to be disbanded and distributed among other squadrons because of their inability to resume the inhumane presuppositions of war.

There must be a better way

Just because Goggins, Willink and Pressfield preach the message of increasing self-discipline at all costs, doesn't mean it is true or wise or that you should follow their advice. And while they may try to convince you and themselves that this strategy is working for them, they are not clear about the catastrophic costs involved at the same time. Although they prove it is possible to manage, suppress, and wage war on their internal resistance and move beyond it, it is madness to preach this logic as the peak motivation strategy for all people.

Thankfully there is a far better way.

2.
The great misunderstanding

Although self-discipline is culturally celebrated as the most important resource for successful humans, it is also the only tool in the shed for most people. Having a bunch of ultra-masculine, ex-military, hard arses preaching self-discipline or die, is only making it harder for the average person to genuinely improve their life.

The underpinning logic of self-discipline is that there is an inherently unmotivated, lazy, weak, or bad part of you that will ruin everything if given half a chance. This belief makes it impossible to rest. If you snooze, you lose. If you are not driving things forward, you are being sucked backwards.

The worst part of the self-discipline strategy is that due to this presupposition about your corrupt nature you must use your best energy against yourself to stay in the game. Parts of you are now at war. War means one side is winning while the other side is losing with inevitable collateral damage for both parties. Therefore, self-discipline is incredibly inefficient. It is a young person's game because it requires you to have energy to waste.

Self-discipline works when you are young because you do have an abundance of energy. You have more than you need. You can afford to be wasteful. You can get away with system inefficiencies. You can steal from Peter to pay Paul and get away with it. However, as you enter the mid-life season, you'll notice you no longer have energy to waste which means you must learn to be much more efficient.

Mid-life success always comes from optimisation and increasing the efficiency of your system. The logic demands that working with yourself instead must be a better way. In fact, until you understand exactly how to do this, the adversarial internal relationship will lead to sabotage and your goals will always be blocked.

The mid-life pinch point

The motivation and performance problem you are trying to solve is not due to a lack of discipline. In fact, at this point, more discipline does more damage than good. Your real problem is a lack of permission – from yourself.

2. The great misunderstanding

The best thing about getting to midlife is that most people are exhausted by the rhetoric of 'try harder' and 'be better' and ready for an alternative. Because self-discipline is so widely celebrated as best practice for internal motivation, and the costs of this approach appear to be negligible, rarely is there a reason to question this method until it all comes crashing down in the mid-life season.

For those who have not already completely supressed their humanity and shut off all possibility of an integrated relationship with themselves, here's what typically happens.

The part of you that has been supressed, accused, mistrusted, dominated and feared has had enough of being treated this way. The deep love and wisdom that resides in your being has now seized the opportunity your exhaustion has provided to demand a conversation about the state of your relationship. While this part of you has suffered in silence for many years, the maximum tolerance level has been reached and the game has now changed for good.

This threshold moment shows up as some kind of increased internal resistance manifesting as a loss of energy, drop in motivation, procrastination, lack of clarity, brain fog, or self-sabotage (at best) or some kind of major injury, chronic illness, severe physical pain, or autoimmune disorder (at worst) depending on how much fight you have left in you before you are ready to listen.

It is as though fuses are being pulled out of the power box and electricity has been cut off to previously high functioning applications. (The exact symptoms Stuart described in the opening story.)

The safety officer

Another way of conceptualising what is going on, is to imagine your unconscious mind is like the safety officer in charge of workplace health and safety and has stepped on site to demand all work to stop. Clipboard in hand, there are a list of severe safety breaches requiring urgent attention before production can resume. While it may appear that you are being thwarted by your inner 'bitch' who hates the idea of things going well for you, considering the importance of safety in your life will give you cause to reconsider.

Whether you like it or not, every cell in your body is hardwired for self-protection. When in danger (real or perceived) we instinctively activate full defence protocols as part of the nervous system's flight / fight response. We only protect that which we value, so self-preservation is evidence of genuine self-love. The safety officer is your friend. They want productivity and success as much as every other part of you, it's just that your operations must be safe. You can't just turn off your need for safety.

Permission denied

The central dilemma you now face is that whether you like it or not, **you do NOT have permission from yourself to move forward in life under these current arrangements.** As a result, all progress and production is being actively resisted. The handbrake is firmly on and no matter how hard you try to forge on, you cannot. This is not because there is anything wrong with you, it is simply a loving restriction from your unconscious mind because certain aspects of your current set up are not safe.

More courage and less fear is yesterday's game. That logic may work while you are young, but good luck running that strategy now your unconscious has found its voice.

If you were to have permission to fully show up and maximise your energy and focus without addressing the safety concerns, that would be reckless and lead to certain calamity. However, once you address the necessary requirements to make your life safe again, then the handbrake is released, and you are free to power-up!

Leverage against yourself

The message of my last book, *Leverage*, was that there comes a time when the space between two people has become so polluted that change must happen. The issue is that two people are never ready for change at the same time. Someone must go first. It falls to the person with a clearer grasp of their desired future or the greater felt pain of the present state of affairs to do something about it. It is only when one party feels the current situation is untenable, reaches a limit and then reluctantly demands an honest conversation to sort things out that the relationship can be improved.

When it comes to marriage, there is no reliable way to predict which partner will be the one to lead the change conversation, but in your own relationship with yourself, I can guarantee that in the mid-life motivation pinch point, it will always be your unconscious mind to demand the change.

The airing of grievances will quite predicably be some version of this spray below:

> "OK can you stop being such a jerk please?
>
> Yeah, I know Goggins is a freakin' legend and Willink is a beast. Yes, I know Pressfield has been on the Joe Rogan

show and Tim Ferriss says his book is a must read. I get that you've been able to dominate me through the strength of your will and get shit done even when you don't feel like it. That's all great. Really impressive stuff. But can you see that you've treated me like your enemy this whole time using your will power to dominate, force and fight against me? I've been gracious knowing its only out of fear and ignorance that you think this way, but I can't keep going like this. I'm not prepared to be seen as your enemy for a moment longer. That's bullshit. It's unfair. I'm not OK with it anymore!

And here's the thing...I've been playing along and tolerating your leadership because you just weren't ready to stop and change. You were doing too well with your 'dominate and conquer' strategy to listen to an alternative. But now things have changed. You are tired and worn down from the battle. Now is my chance. If you'd like to continue treating me poorly and perpetuating the misunderstanding any further, then I'll actually be your enemy. I will dial up the resistance with greater intensity, resourcefulness, and power. I will get in your way. I will thwart all your plans and remove all my support from your goals. I'm stronger than you. I will beat you. You don't actually want to go to war with me no matter how convincing Pressfield may seem."

As Carl Jung says, "If we understand anything of the unconscious, we know that it cannot be swallowed. We also know that it is dangerous to suppress it, because the unconscious is life, and this life turns against us if suppressed, as happens in neurosis."[9]

Your unconscious mind now has leverage to MAKE you do what you wouldn't or couldn't do otherwise. This is a pure example of 'changing the people you love for all the right reasons to get the relationships you deserve'. (The subtitle of the Leverage book if you are not familiar with my work on relationships).

---

[9] https://artsofthought.com/2020/11/17/carl-jung-and-the-shadow-a-guide-to-the-dark-side-of-the-mind/

3.
Self-permission

If self-discipline is energy against yourself, then self-permission is the complete opposite. It is to work with yourself and have all your thoughts, emotion and energy pointed in the same direction.

Self-discipline is a limited resource dependant on poor self-awareness and a terrible relationship with yourself. Self-permission is a limitless resource based on a repaired and fully functional relationship with yourself.

Here is a summary of some of the key differences between the two self-motivation strategies from my book, *Unhindered*.

SELF DISCIPLINE	SELF PERMISSON
A behaviour management strategy. It only deals with the end product never the production line. Therefore, it will only produce short-term gains.	Focuses on changed beliefs which then automatically change the behaviour. It deals with the production line, not the end product.
A childish form of motivation. It requires no self-awareness or maturity and works only because you have energy to waste. It is the kindergarten version of trying to do your best work.	The adult form of motivation. As such, it allows you to access the best of who you really are and what you're capable of. It's an incredibly efficient and effective use of energy.
Based on the fear that you are weaker than you think.	Demonstrates that you are far stronger than you imagined.
Driven from the conscious mind. It pays no attention to the realm of the subconscious.	Accesses unconscious wisdom, intuition and knowing. It aligns your whole being to be pointed in the same direction.
Requires you to fight, dominate and control yourself to win. It feels like you must climb the snow-capped mountain to capture the flag.	Requires you to listen, trust, forgive, and accept yourself. It's releasing the handbrake to allow yourself to flourish and naturally move towards your goals.
Cruel and unnecessary. It ultimately violates your relationship with yourself and can lead to trauma.	It is 10 times more powerful and a sustainable form of motivation. It is a kind and loving way to access the best of you.
MASSIVLEY OVERRATED	**ALWAYS WINS**

©Jaemin Frazer 2019

How permission works

When you were a kid, everything you wanted was on the other side of permission. Adults held the permission that always required you to behave in certain ways to receive it. Permission was often denied by these adults if they were unhappy with you.

> *Can I go to the toilet miss?*

> *Not until you've finished your maths questions.*

> *Can I go to the party Dad?*

> *No way, you haven't mown the lawn like I asked you to.*

Most adults are still craving this permission, and performing for it, just as they were as a child.

If you don't understand how self-permission works, you set up some very dysfunctional and external way of still trying to get permission from the grown-ups:

- You'll find the permission to rest only when you are sick. Therefore, you'll need to be sick every time you need a break from your unsustainable life.

- You'll find the permission to fully try your best only when you are completely backed into a corner and where everything is against you. Therefore, you'll keep sabotaging your life through procrastination, avoidance, and mistakes, to create the only space you have permission to perform.

- You'll find permission to change only when approaching a culturally accepted milestone. Therefore, you'll only notice in yourself a sense of anticipation that builds towards milestone numbers or special dates on the calendar.

- Or you'll find permission to be content with your life only when you feel that God is happy with you, and you are living in alignment with his will.

We all want to live a meaningful and fruitful life, it's just that, without even fully realising it, most people are still inadvertently looking to be granted permission externally. This takes the form of seeking approval from friends or family, seeking a sign from God, waiting for the stars to be aligned, hoping for a miracle, placing weight on superstitions, or waiting for special dates and arbitrary milestones.

When you realise that permission is an adult's job and you are the adult in your life, you no longer are required to wait for anyone or anything to give it to you.

You are now the permission giver. Permission is your job.

Sure, there are still requirements to be met for permission to be granted, but now you have the key to unlock the door from the inside.

Permission must be granted

Perhaps the most important concept in this entire book is that permission always comes with prerequisites.

Here it is in a sentence:

Permission is only granted when all required conditions are satisfied.

Self-permission is no different.

Just like the child cannot just give themselves permission to go the toilet or the party without the adults agreeing, you cannot just give yourself permission to be happy or successful without being released to do so by your internal safety officer. ***There are conditions to be satisfied first.***

To override the rules or ignore the conditions and just do it anyway, always ends badly.

I often hear people misuse the term self-permission in this way.

You cannot simply give yourself permission to rest, not care what others think about you and move confidently into the thing you want to do with your life, when your whole strategy for life is built on a childhood operating system with a bunch of critical safety concerns unable to sustain your adult goals.

If your concept of self-permission is still a form of managing yourself to override your common fears, dysfunctions, and patterns of poor behaviour, then you've completely misunderstood how it works.

This is still self-discipline energy.

You still do not trust your nature.

You still are afraid that the worst part of you will take over and ruin your life if you are not careful.

True self-permission is granted from your unconscious as soon as you satisfy the safety concerns, not forced from the conscious mind trying to get you to move ahead no matter the cost.

Granted, the term is easily misunderstood, but the essence of self-permission is responsible safety. Your success must also be safe. Until your internal world is safe, your instinctive need for safety will show up as resistance and a strong NO. You will have to fight against this safety mechanism to make any progress. If you are some kind of superhuman, or if you still have the abundant energy of youth, you may succeed momentarily, but in every other case it is pure madness to imagine this is a sustainable plan for a successful life.

Again, let me make this as simple as possible.

Permission to move forward into the life you desire is granted from the unconscious when the safety concerns of your current internal operating system have been completely addressed and upgraded.

Do you have permission?

To get you started down this line of thinking, take a moment to ask these counterintuitive questions of yourself.

- If you are trying to lose weight, do you have permission to be attractive?

- If you are trying to promote yourself, do you have permission to stand out?

- If you are trying to share your message, do you have

permission to speak up?

- If you are trying to improve your financial situation, do you have permission to be wealthy?

- If you are trying to stop working so hard, do you have permission to rest?

- If you are trying to find a partner, do you have permission to be in a romantic relationship or fall in love?

If the answer is 'no', then no matter how hard you push yourself to get these things anyway, you will always be internally resisted. Until you address the significant safety concerns with getting the things you desire, permission will be lovingly denied.

Thankfully these safety concerns are entirely predictable.

4.
The Four Safety Concerns

To solve the safety problem, there are four general conditions that will need to be fully satisfied until permission to move forward is granted and the resistance is removed. These conditions represent the biggest safety breaches for every mid-lifer who has not updated their internal operating system.

This is a universal and predictable problem for all ambitious mid-lifers. Ultimately, you'll only know I'm right when you apply what I'm suggesting, and it works.

Here is an explanation of each of the four conditions as they are listed on the safety officer's board:

1. You don't trust yourself

2. You keep showing up needy

3. Your gameplay sucks

4. You have incongruent avatars for each game that you are playing

I'll explain precisely why these four issues are major safety concerns and how to make the necessary upgrades to your operating system. But, before I do that, you can take the self-permission test now to see how you currently score against each of these 4 safety issues.

www.jaeminfrazer/selfpermission

5.
Safety concern number one: You don't trust yourself

Red flag number one is that you do not trust yourself. This makes the top of the safety breach list because this lack of trust within is the single most dangerous aspect of your life.

While you may feel this is unfair or untrue, behaviour never lies. If you genuinely trusted yourself, you could not behave the way you do.

Many people are not familiar with the feelings of self-trust because of how focussed they are on pretending they are confident to others. Yet, the more you try to prove your own self-worth outwardly the less you are actively referencing yourself. While it may appear that you back yourself or you may have convinced others you believe in yourself, the further away you are moving from having a genuinely trusting relationship with yourself.

Another common example is when people openly project their lack of trust onto others. While the outward complaint is always about how they can't trust anyone, the real problem being communicated is that they don't trust themselves.

If you've ever had the feeling that everyone is out to get you, no one really cares about you, or those closest to you are always waiting to stab you in the back, have you ever considered that it might actually be yourself that you don't trust?

Here is some further evidence that proves you don't trust yourself:

- Not listening to yourself

- Always seeking out advice from others

- Ignoring your own intuition or sense of what is right.

- Blocking out physical or emotional pain

- Forcing yourself to do what is expected

- Avoiding hard decisions

- Always justifying or explaining your decisions to others to try and convince them you are doing the right thing (when you are really trying to convince yourself)

Managing yourself

The final proof of a lack of trust within is that you are managing yourself. This is likely to be the hardest one to see, yet if you are going to have permission granted, it is essential that you understand the problem with treating yourself this way.

All attempts at self-management can only be seen as evidence that you do not trust your natural ability to achieve your desired results. Similarly, every attempt at self-discipline reveals that you cannot relax in your own natural ability to get what you want. You are trying to make yourself do what does not seem to come naturally in order to succeed. You have to be 'better than', 'other than' or 'different than' you are in your natural state otherwise you fear you will move away from the goal rather than towards it.

Domain specific mistrust

It is important to add that trust, like security, may be domain specific. You may feel totally safe, secure and at ease with your ability to handle any challenge in one domain in your life, yet the moment you step outside of that comfort zone, all trust and safety is gone.

I have a Christian friend who is one of the purest examples I've ever seen of living without fear especially when it comes to money. He does not waste one moment of energy worrying about it. He trusts that money will always be there when and where he needs it, that God has abundantly resourced him to fulfill his calling and that he will be able to lead the organisation to continue getting bigger and better. This is more impressive to me because he is running a large organisation with a huge budget and is constantly looking to grow the scope and size of the work they are doing. There is always an extraordinary amount of complexity that comes with the territory he occupies, and yet there is still zero fear or anxiety. God will provide and he is doing what he was born for. He does not ever make decisions based on fear in this space.

And yet, take him out of his safe world, and there is an abundance of dangers to be afraid of. The democrats, the misinformation on social media, the sexual content on YouTube, alcohol, swearing, pop music, pornography on the internet, drugs, crime, and the state of the world. So, in every other domain of his life, there is no trust and maximum fear. He is driven to protect his children from the dangers of the world by cloistering them away where he can monitor their exposure to any potential hazards.

He can point to the logic of his fears by describing the historic alcoholism in his extended family, the pain caused by affairs, and children born outside of marriage. He feels justified in his concerns for his daughters in an increasingly sexualised world, but more for his sons that lust will ruin them as it has so many other Godly men, and even church leaders. Under scrutiny, he trusts his fences not his nature. His world is very managed and his children very controlled.

He simply does not trust himself in the real world because he's assumed that the sins of his family are evidence of a deep flaw within them and also within himself.

The evidence is clear. He does not trust himself.

The problem is that it is a dangerous way to be a human.

Case closed

Imagine you've got oversight of a team of people with an important project to deliver on. You may say that you trust your team to deliver, but when asked about your leadership style, everyone rolls their eyes. You ride your people. You micro-manage them. You threaten to fire them when they underperform. You pretend to listen to their concerns and requests so that they feel valued and understood, but then you just do it your way anyway – because you know best. You string them along with the lure of performance incentives but keep moving the goalposts so that they keep giving all they've got. Basically, you are a pain to work for. Your team do NOT feel motivated to perform for you. They know you DON'T trust them no matter what you say, and they are moments away from sabotaging your business or telling you to stick the whole thing 'where the sun doesn't shine' and walking away for good.

In case you missed the metaphor, your conscious mind is the boss in this story, and the team is all that is unconscious inside you.

The verdict is in. You do not trust yourself even though you may have been unaware or pretending this is not true for most of your life.

While you may never have fully considered the importance or even possibility of self-trust, having a lack of trust within your relationship with yourself is incredibly dangerous. If there is no safe place within yourself to retreat to, the world will eat you alive.

How do you expect to survive in the world following your heart's desire without implicit trust. It's just not safe. If you don't trust yourself, how is anyone else expected to? You are a danger to yourself, and the world, and must be restrained and managed. No wonder you do not have permission to move forward right now.

The golden thread – Trust is essential

For some readers, it's probably no surprise that lack of trust is the first item on the safety red flag list. The idea of trusting yourself is a core element of collective wisdom spoken of by spiritual teachers through the ages. Additionally, the contributions from modern thought leaders on the subject clearly demonstrate that without trust within yourself, you have nothing.

In his book – *The Miracle Equation*, Hal Elrod teaches that the formula for the seemingly supernatural is to combine unwavering faith with extraordinary action. For this to happen, you must trust your vision, trust your destiny and trust in your ability to bring it into being.

In his book *The Power of Intention*, Wayne Dyer teaches that magic happens when you align yourself with the seven faces of intention. This cannot happen until you trust the universal spirit of intent is all around you and to trust that you are also by your very nature part of this spirit of intention.

Napolean Hill in his classic work, *Think and Grow Rich*, says that there has been more gold mined from the thoughts of men then there has ever been from the earth. However, plenty of good ideas have died with those who thought them, because it is not until you are willing to trust the quality of the idea completely and inexorably, and your ability to bring it to bare, that one can see their dreams fulfilled.

In William Whitecloud's book, *The 7 Secrets of Magic*, he gives perhaps the most compelling and clear explanation of this truth that there is no possible way of achieving your dreams until you trust your natural ability to achieve the results you desire. Whitecloud vividly demonstrates the stark difference between what happens when you trust your natural ability to achieve the results you desire as opposed to when you get stuck focusing on what you need to do to get what you want instead.

I consider each of these works among the best books I've read and the most important wisdom available to each of us on the subject of achieving our true potential. However, the one missing piece in each of these brilliant books is an effective strategy of HOW to completely restore trust within yourself when it has been lost, damaged or broken.

5. Safety concern number one: You don't trust yourself

Of the authors mentioned above, William Whitecloud gives the most attention to this question, although his answer still falls remarkably short. Here is a summary of his approach starting with the first two secrets of magic:[10]

Secret 1. Your thoughts and feelings aren't real. Your thoughts and feelings are an expression of your underlying assumptions in any moment, not a reflection of actual reality or what is truly possible and,

Secret 2. Your focus creates your reality. Your experience in life is determined by what you put your attention on. If you focus on end results you inevitably attract what you want. If you focus too much on what you must do to get what you want, you end up attracting your doubts, fears and beliefs.

Whitecloud teaches that trust is built in the present moment with a conscious decision. When trust goes missing, he directs readers to name what they are afraid of, see that their thoughts and feelings are not actually real and simply move back to trusting their nature again.

He advises that reviewing the wounds of your past where trust has been broken or betrayed before, is entirely

---

10 The Magicians Way – William Whitecloud. New World Library, California, 2009, Page 233

unnecessary. All you need to do is simply decide to completely trust yourself here and now.

While I entirely agree with the prerequisite of trusting your nature as the foundational truth that magic is built upon, the strategy of simply dismissing all the years of accumulated, repeated thoughts and feelings that undermine trust is not a believable plan.

To emphaise how unbelievable this strategy is, the 7th secret of magic explains the role our hearts play in us experiencing the life we truly desire.

Secret 7. It takes will. 'Ultimately, your highest source of energy is your own heart. Yet, the paradox is that you are conditioned to protect your heart, a behaviour motivated by fear. Your fears are communicated to you by thoughts and feelings. There can be no sustainable change in your experience of life unless you have the will to choose what's in your heart instead of resolving the tension of your thoughts and feelings by escaping into comfort.' [11]

The problem with this logic is that the seventh secret cannot be fully embraced until you've ended the war with your assumptions and healed your own heart completely.

---

11   The Magician's Way – William Whitecloud. New World Library, California, 2009, Page 235

5. Safety concern number one: You don't trust yourself

If your thoughts and feelings are simply an expression of your underlying assumptions that there is a problem within, and you cannot afford to just trust your nature to lead you towards what you want, then to just tell yourself that these thoughts and emotions aren't real so you do not have to listen to them, will not be enough to break the loop in your head and heart. You will constantly have to manage your thoughts and emotions in every situation.

It would make more sense to dissolve the loop completely by confronting the underlying assumption all the way back to the first time you decided it was true. Then you wouldn't have to manage your thoughts and feelings all the time. There would be nothing to manage!

And, more importantly, while you might call it an assumption now, it has been stored in your psyche as bed rock certainty and core truth. It feels more real than anything else. It is not easily dismissed as nothing! So, to say, just focus on what you want and don't worry about any thoughts and feelings that come up when these very thoughts are screaming at you saying that you can't have what you want because of what you truly believe about yourself, is in no way believable.

To trust yourself completely will require you to completely dissolve the cause of your mistrust.

It takes time

Another flawed misconception, often accepted as wisdom, is that it always takes time to rebuild trust.

This idea does not hold up under scrutiny either. Broken trust is a safety issue. And since every cell in our body is hardwired for self-protection, safety issues cannot simply be ignored or turned off no matter how much time has passed.

Imagine agreeing to trust someone again who'd significantly hurt you in the past, without any conversation about the thing they did that betrayed trust in the first place. Even if you truly desire to move on and you genuinely love and care about this person unconsciously you can't help but be guarded towards them. If they have betrayed you once and have not fully reconciled that experience with you, part of you fears they will do it again. Trust is not naturally or automatically rebuilt over the course of time. This person is still a danger to you and therefore wisdom dictates you must remain guarded towards them.

You cannot completely trust someone without dealing with the danger first.

Can you be trusted though?

Concluding that trust is central to a successful life is one thing, but this logic instantly falls apart if the problem with you is that you are not trustworthy and therefore cannot be trusted in the first place.

If self-discipline is built on the assumption that you can't be trusted because of an inherent problem inside your core, the only way to move away from this accepted self-discipline strategy must be to explore the base assumptions with your nature, and while we are at it, the basic elements of all human nature.

What is at your core? Are you inherently good or bad? What does it mean to be human? Can you be trusted?

To do justice to answering these existential questions, allow me to examine the work of those who've tried to do so in the past.

The Christian answer

All attempts at managing yourself through self-discipline are proof that you believe you cannot be trusted. The only reason you believe you cannot fully be trusted is because there must be a problem with your nature. Your natural, unmanaged state is a danger to yourself and others. The reason you are convinced this is true is because your answer to the question about why you've behaved poorly in the past has been influenced by the accepted wisdom that has been absorbed into the collective consciousness. In the western world, the single loudest voice shaping the collective consciousness about human nature has been the church. Whether you consider yourself religious or not, you may be quite surprised to discover how deeply Christian thinking about human nature has infiltrated your psyche.

Let's start by examining two of the most revered Christian writers on the subject of human nature: The Apostle Paul and Saint Augustine.

The Apostle Paul

The Apostle Paul is generally regarded as one of the most important figures of the Christian church. Fourteen of the twenty-seven books in the New Testament have traditionally been attributed to him, and his teachings continue to be vital for all Christians.

As a Jewish lawman, Paul was violently against those following the way of Jesus. He killed, tortured, and persecuted many people in the name of defending the Jewish tradition from the Christian sect. However, one

5. Safety concern number one: You don't trust yourself

day when traveling to Damascus, he was knocked from his horse by a blinding light and confronted by what he describes as the voice of Jesus himself. This becomes the major pivotal point in his life and caused an instant transfer of allegiance. In a single moment Paul changed from being the number one persecutor of Christians, to the number one propagator of the faith.

In his letter to the church in Rome he grapples with the logic of how he could have behaved so differently then and now.

Of his former life, he says:

> "It is I who am carnal and have sold my soul to sin. In practice, what happens? My own behaviour baffles me. For I find myself not doing what I really want to do but doing what I really loathe…I often find that I have the will to do good, but not the power. That is, I don't accomplish the good I set out to do, and the evil I don't really want to do I find I am always doing."[12]

Paul says, look, I want to do good things, but I can't because I have a natural and unavoidable inclination towards doing the wrong thing.

---

[12] Romans 7:14-20

> "Wretched man that I am, who will deliver me from the body of sin? Thanks be to God who delivers me through Jesus Christ our Lord."[13]

Two natures

Paul then continues to rationalise why he behaved in ways that is now abhorrent to him by introducing the idea of two natures. He teaches the early church that they are born with a sinful nature that cannot do good and then they received a new spiritual nature which sets them free from their natural desire to do the wrong things after being born again through accepting the sacrifice for sin made by Jesus.

This becomes a battle of flesh versus the spirt. He says:

> "Those who live according to the flesh have their minds set on what the flesh desires, but those who live in accordance with the Spirit have their minds set on what the spirit desires...but those who are in the realm of the flesh cannot please God...Therefore, brothers and sisters, we have an obligation – For if you live according to the flesh you will die, but if by the Spirit you put to death the misdeeds of the body you will live."[14]

---

13 Romans 7:24-25
14 Romans 8:5-14

5. Safety concern number one: You don't trust yourself

In his reflections searching for an answer about how he could have been so governed by his base desires, what is most concerning is that he throws his hands up declaring that his own behaviour *baffles* him.

Paul, the founding father of Christian thinking says that his poor behaviour is a mystery and so is left to guess the root cause. He doesn't know why he behaved the way he did but assumes it can only be because his nature must be sinful, meaning, left to his own devices, he can only do wrong.

The problem here is that Paul's guess forms the basis of his instructions to everyone else battling with the same conundrum. Everyone has had experiences where they too have done things they didn't want to do, and not done the things they knew they should do!

Because Paul became elevated within the early church, his words became immortalised. Paul must be right about his own nature because he is Paul, and if Paul is right about his nature, then he must be right about my nature as well.

Now his guess about his own baffling behaviour becomes the accepted and unchallenged wisdom for billions of people worldwide 2000 years later. That means most of the earth's population are still deeply governed by Pauls wrong answer to the right question.

Can you be trusted? Paul says NO.

Saint Augustine

Saint Augustine (13 November 354 – 28 August 430) was a theologian, philosopher, and the Bishop of Hippo, in Roman North Africa. His writings have greatly influenced the development of both western Christianity and western philosophy, and he is viewed as one of the most important Church fathers. His many important works include *The City of God, On Christian Doctrine*, and *Confessions*.

Like Paul, Augustine had to reconcile two distinctly different seasons of his life. He describes his teenage years as a "bubbling cauldron of vice" and then when he later became a Christian, he lived a life of monk-like celibacy and was a model of uprightness and virtue.

In his autobiographical book *Confessions*, in which he outlines his sinful youth and his conversion to Christianity he explains that as a wild young man, he had an awareness of God and the ways of the church but found great enjoyment in doing whatever he pleased instead. While he occasionally had pangs of conscience, he would pray "Lord, make me pure — but not yet!"

5. Safety concern number one: You don't trust yourself

Augustine hinges his argument about his nature, and therefore all of human nature, on a story from his youth about stealing pears. While kicking around with his teenage friends, he and his mates took a bunch of pears from a farmer near where they lived. They knew it was wrong yet spurred each other on to do it anyway. In his later reflections about this incident, Augustine concludes that the only possible motivation for their behaviour was the pure pleasure of doing wrong. From this conclusion he taught that there is a part of our nature that enjoys the thrill of wrongdoing, just for the sake of its own badness. We delight in sin, from a tiny pointless lie, or a nasty put-down, all the way up to adultery and betrayal. Augustine agreed with Paul's assessment that we are born sinful and to describe this problem with our nature, introduced the term 'original sin' for the first time.

For this reason, Augustine says even more loudly than Paul – No you cannot be trusted.

Guilt becomes good

From the foundational teachings of Paul and Augustine, the late English writer and philosopher, Alan Watts says, that the church has institutionalised guilt as a virtue.[15] The more focussed you are on your guilt and shame and how worthless

---

15   https://alanwatts.org/transcripts/jesus-his-religion/

a sinner you are, the more spiritual and Godlier you are considered. In this way, the church rewards your awareness of bad behaviour far more than any good behaviour you may produce. Ironically good behaviour is then blatantly discouraged as self-righteousness and works of the flesh.

When a Christian does do anything kind, generous or pure, they must point to the love of God as the source of their good behaviour and continue mistrusting their own motives and desires outside of Christ.

The bible is wrong

What if we were to re-read Paul and Augustine's writings for what they really are – two good men trying in vain to understand and reconcile the incongruent behaviour of their past.

Both Paul and Augustine conclude that bad behaviour is pure evidence of being a bad person.

But is this the only story that can be told about stealing pears or persecuting the first Jesus followers? Would a dispassionate observer place the same meaning on it? Is there any other logic to what could motivate a young man to steal pears other than for the delight of doing wrong? Is there any other data that proves beyond doubt that he is inherently wicked or is that it?

Although many would loudly proclaim that centuries of evidence of evil human behaviour only solidifies the biblical wisdom of Paul's words and proves him right, all the evidence is based on a faulty presupposition that has no substance when scrutinised.

My attempt at deconstructing and summarising Paul's writing is done as one who gave absolutely everything to living as though these words are the purest, wisest, most spiritual way of understanding and overcoming the innate battle between good and evil.

I lived and breathed Paul's words. As a Pentecostal Christian church pastor for 10 years, I preached this ideology wholeheartedly and plumbed the depths of this way of living for myself and the world around me.

I never imagined that his words would not be the ultimate guide to living the life I desired.

When the coaching framework gave me cause to re-examine the presuppositions underpinning my thinking and the non-negotiables governing my logic, I saw the world in dimensions that I'd been locked out of.

When you are tied to certain fundamental ideas as non-negotiable truth, then you must distort all experience to fit your map of the world.

This becomes a self-fulfilling and inescapable loop: I am bad to my bones, so I need the biblical answer to my greatest problem. The bible is true, so, if it is giving instructions about what to do with my sinful nature, then I must be correct about my own self-assessment.

Paul's writings are great if you are trying to solve the problem of what to do with your sinful nature. But as soon as I'd freed my mind from the previous logical loop, I considered new possibilities, and discovered that a foundational mistake had been made, and Paul's words instantly lost their value.

If the accepted wisdom is that humans are inherently bad, all future experiences and evidence is based upon that foundational assumption. But what happens if that assumption is proven to be false? Then all the evidence stacked upon it falls over too.

Where is this hard evidence of the sinfulness of human nature? Where is the evidence that conclusively demonstrates the heart of man is inherently wicked, selfish and corrupt. All we've got here is a couple of guys having

5. Safety concern number one: You don't trust yourself

a bad guess about why they behaved wrongly. That's all. The problem with them guessing wrong is now everyone else is guessing wrong too.

I know Paul and Augustine are wrong because when I run the same tests, no matter how I crunch the data I cannot reproduce their findings. They just do not stack up. There is no evidence.

When I honestly and objectively reviewed this data in my own life, I cannot find this original sin. It was all a giant misunderstanding. I'm fine actually and always have been. I didn't know this was true, and so got awfully messed up in my own head trying to make sense of my own poor behaviour, but now I see that I was just trying to meet my needs and protect my fears in the best way I knew how.

Since Paul and Augustine's assessment of their own bad behaviour and the subsequent endorsement as their standing within the Christian world as heroes of the faith, men and women henceforth have been terrified of their own bad behaviour and what it means about them. The tragedy is that instead of reviewing the data objectively, they base their whole life and teachings on their faulty assumptions as though they are unquestioningly true.

Just because Paul felt like this, and just because many

people feel similarly, and just because it is in the bible, doesn't make it true. It is all part of the tragic misunderstanding of the human condition.

The Human Condition

I'm sure that every person is on some level aware of a battle between good and evil that plays out inside them. Everyone naturally wants to be seen as a good person, yet at the same time, they are afraid that if they were laid bare and had to give a full account for every decision, behaviour, and hidden motivation, that at their core, they are not good at all. There is evidence that at least part of them is bad.

For fear of that badness ever being exposed or worse still confirmed, people run or hide to never be found out.

The reason people cling to religion is that they are terrified of their nature unmanaged, just like everybody else. Everyone has their own versions of what they do to manage the fallout of what they fear to be true about themselves. Religion is one of the most common and dangerous versions of management strategies. And the most religious are those most afraid of their own nature.

It serves organised religion to preserve and propagate this way of thinking because then people will never trust their own judgment and instead outsource responsibility for their morality and destiny to spiritual teachers – God's representatives given to keep you safe from yourself.

This leads people to believe they should be suspicious of what they want. To trust their nature would lead to inevitable disaster because their nature is inherently bad.

Blessed are the pure in heart

In the famous sermon on the mount, Jesus said "blessed are the pure in heart for they shall see God. (Matthew 5:8)

This should be an incredibly troubling verse for most Christians. If only the pure in heart see God, and the problem with people is that their hearts are sinful and impure, we've got a major problem.

The great thing about this message from Jesus is that it takes you out of religion completely. That's the irony. "Blessed are the pure in heart, for they shall see God!" What if you were to examine your own nature, reconcile the misunderstandings of your childhood, and come to see the original and inherent purity of your own heart?

Then the world opens up for you in an extraordinary way and you find God. The divine, the spiritual world, the source, the essence, life itself. Whoever God is and whatever God is like you find God around you everywhere: inside you, inside others in, in the world of nature, in the world of science, in the world of art, in the world of music. It is a spiritual existence when you trust your nature. That has certainly been my experience and that is why I love this verse so much. Because I trust my own heart, I see God everywhere and in everything.

Two Dogs

This thinking around the problem with human nature has informed the psychology of the whole world. Western civilisation has been built off the Judeo-Christian ethic largely shaped by the writings of the apostle Paul and Augustine. This is true not only for the overtly religious, but this ethic underpins our schools, universities, governments, and judicial system.

If you don't think this has made its way into your thinking, have you ever bought into the story of the two dogs fighting against each other?

> "A man traveling through the mountains came upon an old mountaineer who had two dogs. Both dogs were the same size, and they fought continually. The visitor asked the mountaineer which dog usually won. The old

fellow studied for a moment, spat over the fence, and said, 'The one I feed the most.'

While this story is often falsely attributed to the native American Indians, you can thank Paul and Augustine for this one. An early variation of this story was published in *The Daily Republican* on November 16, 1962. William J. Turner Jr. prefaced a meditation on "two natures within"(Romans 7:18-19) with this illustration. [16]

The white dog = the good part of you and the black dog = the bad part of you. Whichever you feed most will win.

Today we have the black dog institute born from this metaphor. The black dog is depression. The part of you that is sad, dark, insecure, overwhelmed, and anxious. The whole strategy to manage your depression is to starve this dog!

Only Human

Another subtle and almost universally accepted language pattern is in moments of mistake or failure to describe ourselves as 'only human' as a justification for the poor

---

16   https://www.newspapers.com/article/the-daily-republican-the-one-i-feeds/106998481/

performance. To be only human is to be come back to the confines of the problem with our nature.

You will make mistakes and hurt yourself and others all the time because you are only human. You can't hope to behave well all the time and to live in line with your values, because you are only human.

This is not a reference to having core needs that require constant fulfilment, it is a statement that pulls us back to our sinful roots. Remember, there is a problem with your nature. You can't fully be trusted to get it right.

Better or worse?

Someone who had been following my work for some time was curious to know if I thought people were better or worse than they imagine? My instant response surprised her. After more than 15,000 coaching hours with people from all walks of life I unequivocally said that they are better. In every case they are better. Invariably, people assume there is something terribly wrong and they are experiencing the fruit of the self-fulfilling prophecies they've created for themselves, but when they objectively review the data and separate their behaviour from intention, there is no solid evidence to back their fears about themselves. Not once. Never.

The problem is that it is so incredibly easy to misunderstand your own behaviour and, just like Paul, assume that bad behaviour can only be evidence of a bad nature.

The Shadow

Carl Jung, one of the founding fathers of modern psychology and the source of shadow theory explains it like this.

> "Unfortunately, there can be no doubt that man is, on the whole, less good than he imagines himself or wants to be. Everyone carries a shadow and the less it is embodied in the individual's conscious life, the blacker and denser it is. At all counts, it forms an unconscious snag, thwarting our most well-meant intentions… Your shadow self is the dark side of our humanity." [17]

While this may sound completely contrary to my response, if you read on, you'll see we are both saying exactly the same thing.

Many people have taken this quote out of context and as a result, entirely misunderstand Jung's shadow theory about human nature.

---

17   https://www.highexistence.com/carl-jung-shadow-guide-unconscious/

Faulty shadow theory

It is easy to assume that when Jung is describing the shadow self, he is revealing bad parts of our nature. He's not. He simply says the shadow is dark. The night is not bad any more than the day is good. The dark things are the places the light doesn't touch. That's all. When you don't understand part of your nature, it's like you leave it in the dark where the light cannot reveal what it really is.

The problem is that the misunderstood Shadow Theory – that the darkness is bad, is largely accepted as the very best way to think about your own life. It has woven its way into modern culture in very subtle and powerful ways.

When this presupposition of being less good than you want is accepted as inescapably true, then all that can be done is to manage the shadow. Yet the shadow is simply the misunderstood self. When the lights come on and your true nature is fully revealed, you are finally capable of examining the truth about your nature.

Jung goes on to explain his shadow theory in more depth:

> *"The personal shadow is the disowned self. This shadow self represents the parts of us we no longer claim to be our own, including inherent positive qualities. These*

> *unexamined or disowned parts of our personality don't go anywhere. Although we deny them in our attempt to cast them out, we don't get rid of them. We repress them; they are part of our unconscious. Think of the unconscious as everything we are not conscious of. We can't eliminate the shadow. It stays with us as our dark brother or sister. Trouble arises when we fail to see it. For then, to be sure, it is standing right behind us.[18]"*

This means the shadow is made up of the parts of us that remain unobserved. It is the things about our self that we don't like, trust, or understand. These aspects of our personality get suppressed, maligned, and feared. This fear of what we do not understand about ourselves creates great danger in our relationship with ourselves and leads to an inevitable increase in evil in the world.

When the shadow remains unexamined it becomes compartmentalised and can only lead to a Jekyll and Hyde conflict between the ideal you and the real you. The parts of you relegated to the darkness will ultimately take over and consume you. Yet, Jung urges people to see the mistake of assuming the shadow is evil.

Because of the compartmental psychology, Jung says that without fail people behave worse than they think they

---

18   https://scottjeffrey.com/shadow-work/

will. This confuses, embarrasses, and disappoints them, and rather than examine why they behaved this way, they discard and suppress these parts of themselves so that no one will see who they really are.

Integrate your shadow

Jung teaches that "The goal of shadow integration is to not act out of your shadow but to recognize the inherent capacity in yourself for all emotional responses, traits, and behaviours"[19]

He urges people not to be afraid of our ability to make mistakes or get things wrong but learn "virtue through sinning".

He says,

> "It is a bewildering thing in human life that the thing that causes the greatest fear is the source of the greatest wisdom. One's greatest foolishness is one's biggest stepping-stone. No one can become a wise man without being a terrible fool. Through errors one learns the truth, through sin we learn virtue. Meister Eckhart says one shouldn't repent too much, that the value of sin is very great.

---

19   https://www.reddit.com/r/Jung/comments/zyzunl/did_jung_mean_we_are_inherently_evil_or_is_that/

5. Safety concern number one: You don't trust yourself

> *We would not know virtue—what is right and proper to do in life—if we did not also know sin—what divides, destroys or hinders life.* [20]

The term coined by Jung for this work is individuation. This means bringing everything into the light. The key is to understand, value, develop, embrace, integrate, and transcend all aspects of our humanity. It all belongs. We must have the capacity for great destruction, evil, and hatred if we hope to contribute true, good, love and creation.

Deepak Chopra accurately captures Jung's heart on the subject when he says:

> *"One of the futile strategies in dealing with the shadow is that the 'good me' takes aspects of the 'bad me' and stuffs them out of sight. In the end, these stuffed behaviours usually surface with a rage...The split self is the most pernicious illusion. Instead of feeding the shadow by keeping secrets from ourselves and others, by harbouring guilt and shame, or by needing someone to blame, we turn things around and stop projecting, detach and let go, give up self-judgment, and rebuild our emotional bodies. Wholeness overcomes the shadow by absorbing it,"* [21]

---

20   https://jungiancenter.org/bi-polarity-human-nature/#_ftn42
21   https://www.spiritualityandpractice.com/book-reviews/view/19877/the-shadow-effect

Can you be trusted – Carl Jung says maybe. But you must truly understand your shadow first.

Standing on the shoulders of those who've gone before us

Bill Bryson's 'A short history of nearly everything' must be included in the conversation of greatest books ever written. I'm convinced it is his finest contribution to the world and we all owe him a debt of gratitude.

As he explains the development of scientific discovery throughout the ages, one of the overriding themes of his book is how one great man or woman stands on the shoulders of the great men and women who've gone before them. One great scientist used their best thinking to explore the frontiers of discovery, and then the next came along and pushed the discovery further.

Could you imagine a world where some arbitrary law capping further scientific development post the 3rd century locked us out of all current technologies and human advancements? The thought is as preposterous as it is unthinkable.

How is it that religious insights are locked with Paul and Augustine, Mohammad and buddha?

It makes no sense.

We have a moral obligation to continue wrestling with these questions and constantly improving the quality of our understanding of ourselves and the world we inhabit.

So are we good or bad or neither?

To be scientific about my self-permission theory means being willing to be objective about the data. It is one thing to have been able to produce certain results once, but if my findings cannot be replicated using the same methods by someone else, then they are of no value. Sure, I've apparently found a way to upgrade from self-discipline to self-permission and genuinely trust myself, but I could be delusional and misguided.

Regardless of what a scientist thinks they will find or even what they want to find, they must be only interested in what they actually find. For my findings to be of value, they must also work cross culturally. If the model works for one person, it must work for all people.

In my quest of answering the question – can we be trusted; my own bias was towards finding that we are each inherently good. I was sure that was truth, and the only way trust becomes possible. But when I scrutinised my process, it was clear I wanted that to be the answer because of how conveniently it would solve the trustworthiness dilemma.

Most religious people have a bias towards the answer being that we are bad. All evidence to confirm this belief strengthens their conviction that they must not trust themselves and must devote themselves to the path of salvation from their badness instead.

However, the objective data seems to suggest that we are neither good nor bad. Both are artificial and inadequate labels to describe human nature.

Clean data

When morality and theology are removed from the equation it is possible to examine human behaviour through the lens of biology and psychology instead.

There is no disputing that the pursuit of pleasure and the avoidance of pain are hardwired into the human being. Objectively, we move towards what feels good and away from what feels bad. When people lean into the inevitable pain that surfaces in any kind of self-improvement journey, it is not that they've overridden these laws, but the pleasure of achievement, growth and success is greater than the pain they must endure to perform at this level.

Similarly, no one is genuinely trying to make their life worse. Any patterns of self-destructive behaviour are still an attempt to increase pleasure and minimise pain. We each try to have a better experience of life using whatever means are available to us. When it seems all viable options for advancement have expired, then attention must be turned to making sure they don't get worse. When it appears that all those around you are hell bent on ruining your existence, rather than to simply surrender to your fate, a person is still motivated to avoid excess pain by taking control of the destruction themselves. Better to hurt yourself than to be hurt by others if their hurt is inevitable. In this way they inflict pain on themselves as a way of preventing further or worse pain in the future.

In this way, we have the capacity to alter our pleasure and pain associations but not to alter the motivational forces of pleasure and pain themselves.

We will always avoid pain and pursue pleasure which is a useful bedrock truth about human behaviour that helps to separate the motivation from the behaviour itself.

Rather than only having the moral judgment of good or bad to describe behaviour, this understanding adds another perspective to why we do the things we do that is unconnected to morality.

Psychological needs

Beyond the biological needs of food, water, air and shelter, Anthony Robbins summarises the complete range of human needs in his brilliant six core needs model. There are three groups of paradox pairs pulling in opposite directions making up six needs in total.

1. Certainty – The need for safety, control, order, and comfort

2. Variety/uncertainty – The need for adventure, change, surprise, and spontaneity

3. Significance – The need for validation, approval, acceptance, value, and importance

4. Love/connection – The need for belonging, understanding, closeness, and to be seen.

5. Contribution – The need to give back, make a difference, add value, solve problems, and leave a legacy.

6. Growth – The need to expand, achieve, experience, enlarge, explore, develop, attain, and achieve.

5. Safety concern number one: You don't trust yourself

There are also 4 overarching principles which govern how these needs play out in our lives and help us to observe all human behaviour in a clean way.

1. All needs must be met. Each need provides an essential part of what is required to survive life. Unmet needs create a vacuum that must be filled. Therefore, you are either meeting each need resourcefully or unresourcefully. Your conscious awareness of how these needs are being met is not a prerequisite to the meeting of the need itself. Your unconscious will find some way to fill your cup, or you will die.

2. Needs trump values. If you have not developed high quality, adult strategies to meet each need in line with your values, your needs will still be met irrespective of your values. (see principle 1) This is precisely why good people do bad things. Remember, behaviour is a strategy to meet needs.

3. Every behaviour has a positive intent. We are intrinsically motivated to do good to, and for, ourselves. We are always trying to bring peace and comfort. No one is trying to ruin their own life. Behaving in ways that hurt ourselves and others is NOT evidence of inherent evil. We do bad things not because we are bad, but because we are needy and haven't found a better way to meet the need (see principle 1 and 2)

4. Change always comes through displacing poor 'need meeting' strategies with better ones. You can't just stop a behaviour if it is meeting a need. You'll simply open the vacuum again. (See principle 1)

Goodness is a function of choice

The more options available to a person seeking to meet their needs, the better their choices become. If you are well educated, financially resourced, in healthy relationships, emotionally mature, and psychologically secure – you will behave in a way that is objectively better than those who have none of these things.

This is crucial in examining human behaviour across the globe. In cultures ravaged by war, corruption, violent crime, oppressive dictatorships and severe poverty, people have so few viable options about how to live and provide for their families and so can be seen behaving in ways that the worlds more fortunate citizens would never even consider.

As Jung says, when fully examined, we are each capable of a great range of behaviours. We have the capacity to do anything and everything. To love and to hate, to raise up and tear down, to heal and to kill, to be kind and to be cruel, to be selfless and selfish. A simple review across the planet at any one point in time would reveal the absolute best and

5. Safety concern number one: You don't trust yourself

worst of human behaviour. In any one case it is possible to say conclusively that people are inherently good just as much as people are inherently bad. There are good people and bad people.

But, if the truth is that we are neither good nor bad at our core, then it must come back to choice. What will I do with what I've been given. As Victor Frankl says in his book *Man's Search for Meaning*, surely the most wonderous ability humans possess is that we get to choose our response to whatever happens to us no matter what is going on around us.

So, if you and I can do things that cause great damage to ourselves and others, then to choose not to is an act of goodness. For good to actually be good, requires the opposite option to also be available. The universe exists in polarities. Light and dark, good and bad, positive and negative. If everything must be good, then how can you call it good? It is ONLY good because it could have also been bad. If you have to love someone, then how can you call it love? It is only truly love because you chose it.

Good and bad are also entirely relative depending on the rules of the game you are playing. A good soldier kills many men to protect many more. A bad soldier cowers in fear while the enemy advances. A bad farmer allows his stock to starve to death in a drought while a good farmer ends their life humanely.

We are real

So, the wonderful conclusion I have come to about human nature is that we are real. It all belongs. The key is to understand, value, develop, embrace, integrate, and transcend our entire experience of life.

The behaviours that people are most bewildered or ashamed about are simply the unreconciled shadow. And those who fear their shadow, end up feeding it.

What makes me certain that I am trustworthy is that I am not afraid of my nature. I know I could do both good and bad in any moment, yet why would I choose to hurt myself or others when I have better choices available to me?

I am always moving towards a better experience of life.

So how do we behave without guidance from above?

Religious people who have had their sinful natures washed clean and upgraded to a new spiritual nature, who claim to be motivated to do good in the world by the wondrous love of God, should be objectively better humans than the rest of us.

They are not.

In fact, most religious people would be far better humans without their faith. So often it is the worst part of them. The irony is that it is their faith that frequently dehumanises and disconnects them from the real world. Talk about sport, art, food, pets or kids, and there is a spark in their eyes, but because everything must ultimately submit to their map of the world and be filtered through the story of humans being separated from God, eventually the conversation becomes weird, and the human connection is gone.

Their fear of the sinful nature and obsession with controlling themselves through being super spiritual often makes them boring, fearful, humourless, and supressed. Not only that, but it can also make them limit and even decrease the collective consciousness of those around them with archaic and tribal living.

The five most surprising qualities of genuinely good humans

In my experience, good humans display all five of these qualities: Objectivity, security, pragmatism, ambition, and kindness. Being a religious devotee may lock you out of four of the five.

1. Objectivity

To be objective is to be external and unattached to your own experience of life, even if only for brief moments. Now that's no small task because we come to the world as sense-making creatures. Unconsciously we filter our experience through our senses, and then we attach a meaning based on our interpretation of events. Everything we experience is subjective. This means life is not happening out there, it's happening in here.

Dr. Robert Keegan, chair of adult development at Harvard argues the 'subject-object shift' is the single most important move we can make to accelerate personal growth. Our subjective selves are simply who we think we are, but when we can move from being attached to this identity to having some objective distance from it, we become much more flexible in how we respond to life.

Even though subjectivity is our natural state, we also have the capacity to think about our thinking, to get outside of our own map and observe, analyse, and improve it. Keegan says that every moment spent switching our viewpoint to being outside our own experience, looking back in, is time well spent. It always gives us more awareness and choice. [22]

Despite how difficult it is, the idea of being objective is very central to being a good human because while ever you remain completely subjective, you'll be convinced that your version of life is the only version, and that is 100% real.

Practicing objectivity helps you understand that all we have is story. It gives you the self-awareness required to take your own story less seriously and you understand that you're probably wrong about most things you think! It is this characteristic which allows you to be humbler about your own truth and more respectful of what others see as truth.

Objectivity genuinely softens you as a human being and it makes you much more pleasant to be around. It also gives you so much more choice as to what you're going to do with your life and how you'll improve the quality of your storytelling in a way that is genuinely good for you and those around you.

---

[22] Adapted from 'Stealing the fire' by Steven Kotler and Jamie Wheel. Harper Collins, New York, 2017. Page 38-39

2. Security

To be secure is the result of deeply loving and accepting yourself for who you are. It is to be certain that you are worthy of love and confident of your capacity to create the experience of life you truly desire. If you are a secure human being, you show up with nothing to prove and nothing to defend, meaning you are now free to contribute out of the overflow of this internal certainty.

When you encounter a secure human being, you are also experiencing a loving human being. To be secure, requires a deep level of love and acceptance toward yourself. This internal love cannot help but radiate outwards. If a person knows how to love themselves, they cannot help but understand the nuance of how to have a loving relationship with others as well. Good human beings do not operate from an internal deficit. They are able to love and be loved in a way that is genuine, pure and devoid of hidden agendas.

Security is a central component to being a good human. To be secure means that you trust your own nature. You can relax in the knowledge that you already have everything you need within you, and that you can trust your natural ability to guide you through the challenges of life.

On the other hand, to be insecure is to have no confidence in your natural state. Worse than that, it is to fear that if you just show up as yourself, it will never be enough. Living from a place of unresolved insecurity means all your best energy is directed at proving and defending yourself, completely undermining your scope to contribute to others. You appear needy, arrogant, selfish, or self-consumed. These are certainly not qualities of genuinely good human beings.

Thinking about insecurity as a solvable problem has been the single focus in my life's work. This is my contribution to the conversation on human nature and helping people become good humans.

3. Pragmatism

To be pragmatic is to rank and organize ideas in a hierarchy of what works best. Good humans are always wired this way. They are not governed by tradition, religion, ideology, other's expectations, or judgments about right and wrong; good and bad. They are governed primarily by improving the quality of their beliefs, thoughts and behaviour so that they continue achieving better results.

This is an extraordinary trait to have, because that means they're able to hold things tightly and loosely at the same time.

Being secure, ambitious and motivated to do what works best allows you to be open to someone showing you alternatives to your current thoughts, beliefs and behaviours on any topic.

The moment this happens, they can jettison their former thinking and update to a new and improved approach.

Pragmatic people are always happy to accept wisdom when they find it, no matter what vessel is used to deliver the message. Additionally, they don't have to prove their way is better. Pragmatic people are open, receptive, humble and teachable. They are agile, flexible, and as such, can improve any area of their life with great speed.

Without this trait people show up closed and sure. They rigidly hang onto things that make no logical sense that cause them to be irrational and overly emotional. They tie their identity to their belief structure and become defensive and threatened when these philosophies are challenged.

4. Ambition

Ambitious people have connected with a compelling vision for their life which means they are always trying to do their best and improve themselves. As such, they are constantly motivating themselves towards something valuable, purposeful and meaningful. They have set their sight on something glorious and are willing to suffer in the pursuit of this end.

Genuinely good humans have not shut down the desires of their heart because of how difficult and problematic these desires may seem to those around them. To desire is human and they have remained honest about this fact despite the cost. Ambitious people know what they want. They trust that their most important desires are inherently good and therefore, have given themselves permission to go after the deepest desires of their heart. They have done the work sifting strange and immature impulses from their most honest goals and dreams so they can get to work bringing these dreams into existence and making the world a better place in the process. Ambitious people know exactly what they want and have given themselves full permission to go after these desires until they become reality.

Ambitious people solve important problems, they push through the boundaries of human limitation, they make the impossible possible, they create magic and wonder, and evolve the collective consciousness. Because they are also secure, they are not driven by selfish or egoic motives, only to maximise the gifts they've been given and to fully show up at their best where it matters most.

This strong sense of ambition tempered by the other characteristics of security, objectivity, and pragmatism, definitely adds to the quality of human life and the ability to contribute meaningfully flows out of that. On the other hand, the ability to be a good human is undermined if you've given up, settled with the status quo, are just surviving, half-arsing, or not doing your best.

5. Kindness

Not to be confused with being nice, pleasant, or agreeable – kindness is to bring goodness to bear on the world around you.

Unresolved insecurity, a lack of self-awareness, tying your identity to ideological non-negotiables, giving up on your dreams, tolerating what you don't want and always thinking you are right is never kind to those around you.

Good people have kind eyes, speak kind words, and operate from a kind heart. They take care not to cause unnecessary harm to those around them and are motivated by seeing others doing well.

More than that, they desire to do good because they can.

Trying to make the world a better place even when it is

costly, hard, and motives are often misunderstood, is a genuinely kind gift to bring. Being secure allows them to come into the world with resources for others, they give certainty to others that they too can heal the wounds of their past. This is kind.

Wanting to be the best you can be and having the courage to pursue the deepest dreams of your heart is kind. Being unattached to your own map of reality and being able to empathise with other people's position is kind. Telling the truth is kind. Being able to get over yourself long enough to listen to others is kind. It is this type of kindness that increases the collective consciousness of the planet, and therefore, must be included in the qualities of genuinely good humans.

Goodness is quantifiable

All five qualities dramatically increase the space you get to play in and the number of real-world choices you have available to you. Just as a business coach could run an audit on your business and tell with a high level accuracy how healthy your business was based on how you scored against key performance indicators, it is similarly possible to quantify a person's goodness based on these 5 metrics. It must also be possible to increase one's goodness by developing each quality.

Back to trust

You will not trust yourself until you see evidence of this goodness in your own life too. Now you have a logical way of knowing what goodness is.

The great misunderstanding

The reason that you don't trust yourself is all based on the deep misunderstanding of your core nature first developed in the painful defining moments of your childhood. While your poor behaviour and disappointing mistakes of the past appear to be all the evidence you need to support this thesis, this assumption is a huge misunderstanding without exception. You have not correctly understood your own desires, motivations, and strategies. You've been too quick to judge and too slow to review the data.

While the broken relationship with yourself has somehow managed to survive in the world up until now, the point is that until this relationship is restored and trust rebuilt, you do NOT have permission to move forward into the fulfilment of your goals and dreams.

6.
How to rebuild trust

Restoring trust is not guaranteed with the passing of time, nor can you simply commit to trust yourself from now on. Instead, you must go back to the moment trust was broken in the first place.

Break through the misdirection with keywords

For those who've had years of therapy and have devoted abundant time, money, and energy to healing the wounds of their past only to still feel unhealed, let me show you why. You've just been lost reviewing an unending sea of wrong data. I'm consistently asked about why my approach will reveal something different when so much time has already been given to sifting through the pain of the past. My answer is that you just didn't know what you were looking for. I'm sorry to say that you've been searching for the wrong thing.

This is the difference between experts and amateurs in any field. Be it finding supernovas in the night sky, cancerous skin cells on a body covered with freckles and moles, or conclusive DNA evidence in a 30-year cold case. Experts can get to the stuff that matters with great speed because of how quickly they can rule out all the information that is superfluous. They know where NOT to look.

Watch what happens when you avoid the misdirection of looking at all the things that happened to you and instead examine your part in this mess.

Let me direct your search using just six keywords.

All six words involve action, and you'll notice that in each case you are the one at the centre of this action.

A. Accusation and Betrayal

As I've explained in my book, *Unhindered*, all insecurity is simply an opinion problem. However, while the word opinion is neutral, the kind of opinions formed by children in painful moments are not neutral at all. They are always negative, and personal, and at their worst, come in the form of an accusation.

6. How to rebuild trust

At some inevitable point in your childhood before you were seven you got hurt for the first time. The problem was not the hurt itself, it was the sense you made of the situation. In your childish wisdom not only did you decide that you were the reason things went wrong, but this sense making took the form of an accusation. You pointed your own finger at yourself and accused yourself of being the problem. This accusation was that a specific crime had been committed. You labelled yourself as weak, stupid, worthless, weird, rubbish or some other precise form of inherent badness. As such, it is possible to trace your woes all the way back to a single and precise word.

This accusation is the exact epicentre of the action. From this point, the real tragedy of this experience was that you decided that you could never just be you ever again. From here on, it would have to be you plus or minus something. Be better than you, different than you, other than you. In this way you looked at yourself and judged yourself as bad, wrong, or inadequate. This siding against yourself in your most vulnerable state is an act of deep betrayal that has reverberated through your being ever since. The real you is now locked out in the cold, banished from the world and covered in shame.

B. Agreement and Certainty

Worse still, because of how shocking this experience was, you also decided you had enough evidence to convict yourself without a trial. This accusation stands. You are guilty as charged. You accuse yourself of being the problem and then agree that this is the complete truth. This agreement then fills you with a sense of pure certainty that you now know who you really are. It is true. You are sure.

This certainty comes with its own chemistry that floods your being and infuses the structure of your beliefs into every cell of your body.

Lock it in.

From here on, you are not running experiments or testing a hypothesis. You are only confirming what you already know to be true.

C. Strategy and System

From this moment, you MUST now direct all resources to protecting yourself from anyone else ever finding out who you really are. Love demands safety. The danger is within you. You must protect yourself from yourself. You can never show up as yourself ever again. It is simply not safe. Having separated you from yourself, the 'ideal you' manages the 'real you.' So that you are never found out.

Now everything you do or say is a strategy to cover and compensate for the agreement about who you think you really are. You create personas to transact with the world in a way that gives you a chance of meeting your needs and protecting your fears. You'll soon become convinced that this is who you are because of how much energy you pour into developing and maintaining these personas.

These strategies receive so much creative energy they become the systems you develop for every area of life. People work perfectly. Your results and relationships are exactly as you designed them to be. The systems *you* created are working exactly as you expected them to.

This is the system you designed based on the strategy to protect your fears and meet your needs, based on agreeing with who you originally accused yourself to be. These personas are all a continued act of self-betrayal.

Reverse the order

Change may be a long time coming but it happens in a moment.

Watch what happens instantly when you use precise language to cut through all the layers of misdirection again and reverse the order of the six key words for how you created the limiting beliefs about yourself in the first place.

a) Strategy and System

b) Agreement and Certainty

c) Accusation and Betrayal

Observe the system, see how perfectly it works.

Examine the strategy.

Understand what the system was designed to achieve.

Uncover the central driver.

What are you running and hiding from?

Who did you say you were?

What exactly did you accuse yourself of?

Open the files.

6. How to rebuild trust

Review the case.

Examine the data.

See through the holes in the case.

Bring new evidence to light.

Notice how the old evidence falls apart: A huge mistake was made.

Data was misunderstood and interpreted poorly.

You can then disagree with the accusation.

Prove the charges are false.

Apologise for taking so long to review the data objectively and for the years of betrayal.

Discover and decide what is true about your nature instead.

Wholeheartedly agree with these new truths.

Hold firm while the new agreements are pressure tested.

Experience the chemistry of certainty from being sure about who you really are.

Now there is nothing to prove or defend and no need to run or hide, you are free to direct your best energy towards growth and contribution.

Notice the new system created as the fruit of being free to be at your best where it matters most, unhindered by self-doubt, fear and limiting beliefs.

You are not a victim

Fahmed was 48 when he came to see me. He was well loved by his friends and family, a respected business leader in his community, yet wracked with crippling anxiety.

Although most people thought he was incredibly successful, Fahmed felt like a fraud. He spent most of his time keeping up appearances and obsessing about keeping key people happy. Worse still, he had been too afraid to execute his big dream because of what others might think. He could see the madness of his situation and was desperate for change but had never been able to get to the bottom of his anxiety despite years of therapy.

6. How to rebuild trust

As soon as I introduced the self-permission model, he instantly knew that was exactly why he felt so stuck. He understood the major work was with his lack of trust within his relationship with himself.

When we examined the defining moments of his childhood, looking for the very first time trust was broken, Fahmed felt as though it could have been one of a hundred different pain points. They all seemed catalogued in his mind as overwhelming evidence of who he really was and how life worked out for him when we diverged from what others wanted him to do. However, as soon as he started talking about the loss of his mum as a young boy, it was clear we'd arrived at ground zero.

At 6 years of age, everything changed. His world went from carefree, safe, and loving, to chaotic, terrifying, and dark the moment his mother dropped dead in the kitchen after school one day, suffering a massive heart attack.

For 2 days after, he thought he would die too, such was the pain in his own heart caused by her absence. On the third day after her passing, Fahmed's uncle came and sat with him and explained that he must stop crying now. It was time to be a big boy and grow up. His father was not coping with the death of his wife, let alone a grieving son incapable of caring for himself.

> *"If you don't stop crying, you will cause more pain for your father, and he will die too."*

His uncle's words pierced deep into Fahmed's heart.

Fahmed felt as though a lead blanket had rested on his shoulders and wrapped around his torso in that moment. He instantly stopped crying and did not shed another tear for 40 years. He maintained full composure throughout the funeral proceedings and when family members tried to console him, he directed all their attention onto his grieving father.

Forty years later, this experience still had an extreme amount of emotional charge and Fahmed was visibly shaken just telling me what had happened. It was not a memory he took any pleasure in revisiting or sharing with others. Although he was very aware of how deeply it had changed the course of his life, he felt entirely powerless to do anything about it.

It seemed perfectly logical to him where the precise epicentre of impact was. Although the moment he saw his mother's lifeless body on the kitchen floor was like a bomb going off inside him, it seemed perfectly clear that it was the insensitive instructions of his uncle that that had ruined him.

The problem Fahmed had, was how this experience was

catalogued in his mind as evidenced by the language he used to describe the problem. Throughout our coaching conversations he continually referred to his anxiety as 'that fucking thing'.

> *I'll be doing fine and then 'that fucking thing' just takes over out of nowhere. Every time I get close to reviewing the traumatic experiences of my childhood, 'that fucking thing' stops me in my tracks, and I get taken out of the game for days.*

I explained to him that naming the problem this way was not useful and more importantly not true, worse still because it was named so imprecisely it had turned into a monster that had consumed him[23]

It was not a 'fucking thing' at all. It was simply *his own* accusation and agreement.

While ever it exists in this form in his mind, it will always be untouchable and traumatic. Yet, it is a classic case of misdirection. The real action did not take place in the death of his mother, the inability to cope with his father, nor the harsh words of his uncle. He cursed himself.

---

23 Rule 10 in Jordan Peterson's 12 rules for life is to "Be precise in your speech" for this very reason. He says: "Things that go unnamed will become monsters that consume you."

No one has the power to bless or curse us without our permission. It's not the words spoken to us, or about us, that change our lives, just the ones we agree with.[24]

This is subtle and very easily missed, but the heart of the action right here: Your agreement. Before a belief is formed, you must agree with some point of data being presented. If you disagree, you cannot then believe it is true.

When Fahmed's uncle spoke those words, Fahmed answered the two sense making questions[25] in a split second without even noticing:

1. Why is this happening?

- *I have misunderstood the situation. I thought it was OK for me to grieve, but that can't be right. Clearly, I do not understand the world or myself, or others.*

2. What does it mean about me?

- *That I can never be me again. If I show up as me in my*

---

24 While this is not a direct quote, credit for this brilliant idea comes from Don Miguel Ruiz's book 'The Four Agreements' Amber-Allen Publishing, San Rafael, 1997.

25 I introduce these two questions as the foundation for all childhood sense making in my book Unhindered – The seven essential practices for overcoming insecurity.

> *natural state with my natural emotions and desires, I will hurt or even kill someone. I cannot be trusted to know what is right or what I should do with my emotions. From this day I will supress them.*

The truth is, Fahmed himself was the lead blanket. In an act of betrayal, he sided with his uncle and father and departed from what was right for himself. He moved from being an advocate to adversary in one moment. He *accused* himself of being weak.

> *I am weak. There is an inherent weakness in me that doesn't know how to handle the world appropriately.*

It may have appeared that there was no other choice for Fahmed, and perhaps that is true. However, this is irrelevant when it comes to rebuilding trust. Whether he could have done it any other way is not the point. Fahmed separated from himself to stay safe from the perceived danger within. This does not look like a betrayal in the moment. The true impact can only be seen through the lens of time.

There is no value gained in wishing the child behaved differently. As the 6 year old kid, Fahmed had limited options and was stuck between a rock and a hard place.

But as the adult, he now has limitless options and can only be stuck in the illusion of no choice.

The tragedy is not that the betrayal happened in the first place. That is inevitable and unavoidable. What has ruined Fahmed's life is that he has not gone back and cleaned up the mess the betrayal made.

This is not just Fahmed's dilemma, it is yours too. Everyone has the own version of this childhood accusation and agreement.

I demand a retrial

The weak case you've got against yourself would never stand up in a court of law. Have you not seen CSI Miami? Even if you think someone is the bad guy, you can't just make stuff up about them and hope it will stick. Where is the evidence? The real, undeniable evidence? You have accused yourself unfairly and have been living as though these charges are completely true.

Imagine a spin off TV series about your childhood. Misunderstandings don't go well on crime shows. It's very embarrassing for the detectives when they get to court to find out they've based their entire case on a simple oversight all because they didn't double check the facts. Simple misunderstandings only work on romantic comedies. In fact, it is what most often drives the plot.

Two hotties fall hopelessly in love and enjoy a wonderful season of unbridled romance only for a simple misunderstanding to throw a spanner in the works and drive them apart. She moves back home to Oklahoma, and he joins the Navy. 30 years later they serendipitously run into each other at a county fair and over a corn dog and a cheap beer they have the conversation whereby they explain that things were not as they seemed all those years ago.

> So, you didn't have sex with Cathy?

> No that was my stupid buddies trying to break us apart because they thought I was spending too much time with you.

> Oh…I see. That kind of changes everything.

The misunderstanding is resolved, and their love is rekindled. Happily, ever after.

This is your drama too. You have not accurately understood everything about the moment of pain, sadness or embarrassment that caused the relationship breakdown with yourself in the first place. You've been treating yourself like the enemy and so when you see through the misunderstanding, you'll have some apologising to do.

The five Readies

The process of rebuilding trust can be described as the readiness for these five actions:

1. Ready to be wrong

Because it has been brought to your urgent attention by the safety officer that you do NOT trust yourself, it means you MUST believe some part of you is dangerous, and therefore, must be carefully managed. Until you are ready to be wrong about this assumption and the specific accusation you made against yourself, there is no possible way trust can be rebuilt.

If you are uncertain about exactly what you've accused yourself of, there is always ample evidence within your behavioural patterns. Behaviour never lies. What must you believe to behave this way?

This level of awareness is also the exact starting point in the 7 essential practices for overcoming insecurity. Before you can overcome the fear you must first, name the fear. Exactly what are you running and hiding from? What is this monster that lurks within?

Being ready to be wrong is not a guarantee that you are in fact wrong. It is simply to undermine the certainty you have always felt about the problem with your nature by conceptualising the possibility of a foundational mistake being made. It is to embrace the gift of doubt and realise that all change is preceded by being wrong about something.

As Mark Manson says "Being wrong opens us up to the possibility of change. Being wrong brings the opportunity for growth." [26]

If you are not ready to be wrong, then nothing can be done.

2. Ready to review

As soon as you are willing to accept that you may have made a mistake about you assumption of the danger within, the next step is to be ready to review all the data and explore every possible place this danger could be hiding. Your unconscious mind is daring you to check. Come on. Have a look. Where is this undeniable evidence that I'm somehow bad, wrong and dangerous? Are you ready to be objective about all the data from a lifetime of experiences? More importantly, are you willing to open the file and review the foundational accusation all further evidence is based upon?

Until you are willing to genuinely go back and have a fresh look at the defining moments of your life, you'll always be convinced that there is still some dark part of you lurking in the shadows waiting to ruin your life.

---

26   The Subtle Art of not giving a F*ck. Mark Manson, Pan McMillon, Sydney, 2016, p121

Anthony Robbins' Six core needs model will provide you with the most objectivity in conducting this review and enable you to separate behaviour from intention for everyone involved in the crime scene you are reviewing. (I'll show you exactly how this works in the next chapter).

If you are not ready to review, then nothing can be done.

3. Ready to apologise

If the honest and objective review reveals the historic accusation does not hold up under scrutiny, then to have held this false claim against yourself represents a crime in itself. Your unconscious is not waiting to enact revenge nor beat you with a stick for the wasted years being at war unnecessarily, but you must apologise to yourself for the pain caused by the deep betrayal of self.

Without unnecessarily complicating this model, apologising effectively involves a lot more than just saying sorry. Your apology must deal with the past danger.

Here's how I describe this process in the Leverage book:

> *"When you hurt someone or someone hurts you, it makes sense that trust is lost. The person who has caused the hurt is now dangerous. There must be protection from

them in case they hurt you again. To trust a dangerous person is foolish. It is wise to be guarded instead. Therefore, the idea that it just takes time to rebuild trust is naïve and simply untrue. Often, time makes things worse. The mistrust and guardedness only increase. The person is still dangerous. To let them back in means they could hurt you again at any moment.

The only way to trust someone again is if they are no longer dangerous. The only way a person could no longer be dangerous is if the damage caused to the relationship in the first place is properly fixed. All you need to rebuild trust again is an effective apology. The moment this happens, safety is restored, and the walls can come down." [27]

You must go back and deal with the damage and completely clean the space in the relationship with yourself.

Following the simple structure to saying sorry effectively is a must. There are four logical stages in an effective apology that enables complete reconciliation and trust to be rebuilt.

---

27 Leverage pg129

The 4 stages of an effective apology:

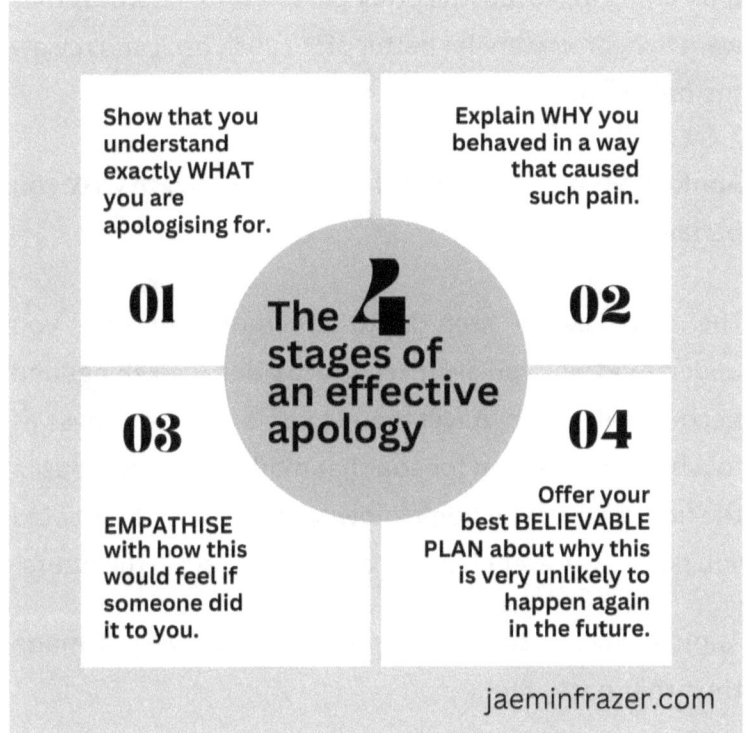

Apology Step 1: Understand and communicate exactly WHAT you did wrong and how that made the other person feel.

To apologise effectively, your first responsibility is to communicate clearly that you accurately understand the mistake made. If you're not sure exactly what you did wrong or why the other person is even upset with you, your apology makes no sense. What are you apologising for?

If you do not agree that the accusation is accurate, rather than trying to placate the other person with the words they want to hear, you are far better off to push back and review the data until you are on the same page.

Apology Step 2: Understand and communicate WHY you behaved that way.

The next logical step is to communicate that you understand why you did it. If you are going to fix things and become safe again, it will require some self-awareness as to what was going on for you that made you dangerous in the first place. If you don't know why you did it, how could you possibly prevent it from happening again in the future?

Apology Step 3: Genuinely empathise for HOW you made the other party feel.

Step three is the place for empathy. Humble yourself, step into the other person's shoes and see how it would feel to have been treated this way. Feel their pain and acknowledge that if someone had done this to you, you would also be hoping for a sincere apology. If you are actually sorry and you want to fix things, now is your chance to show it.

When someone has accepted responsibility for their behaviour and is honestly sad that they've hurt you, it makes it so much easier to accept their apology.

Apology Step 4: Make a believable plan as to why this is unlikely to happen again.

The final step in an effective apology is to talk about the future. Even if you've done the first three steps perfectly, you are not off the hook until you present a believable plan for your future interactions with the person you are apologising to.

To remove guardedness, all we actually need is a believable plan and the sense that it is unlikely to happen again. For this stage to be effective it must be believable to both parties. There is no point overpromising and underdelivering or you will be back apologising again tomorrow. It is your responsibility to put forward a believable plan about how and why things will be different in the future so that the other person can be confident the issue is unlikely to happen again.

Conflict resolution may not be easy, but it's certainly not complicated. When issues are not resolved completely there's an inevitable build-up of resentment, guardedness, and erosion of trust. When these steps are followed, the walls come down, forgiveness can be given freely, and trust rebuilt. The space between you is clean again.

Are we good?

Yeah, we are. Absolutely.

In the context of apologising to yourself, here is how it might play out.

1. What are you apologising for? While the initial accusation is what started the mistrust in the first place, the real crime is not that you betrayed yourself all those years ago, but that it has taken you so bloody long to come back and review the experiences and as such have treated yourself poorly for a long time.

2. Explain why it took you so long to come back in a way that doesn't absolve you of responsibility. Perhaps it is that you didn't know how, or were afraid you were not capable of knowing what to do even if you did go back? Either way you must give a reason for staying away for all these years.

3. Empathise with the part of you that has been misunderstood, maligned, and managed, knowing how much you'd hate it if someone treated you that way. Of course, you will have had numerous experiences of being treated this way by people in your world, so you know exactly how it feels. Make sure you

communicate this emotion with the part of you that has been hurt for so long.

4. Offer a believable plan about why this can't happen again. While you can't promise to never accuse yourself with negative thoughts or words, you can commit to never *agreeing* with these words and therefore never betraying yourself again. As the protestant reformer Martin Luther famously said.

> "*Dear brother, you cannot prevent the birds from flying in the air over your head, but you can prevent them from building a nest in your hair*".[28]

A full four stage apology will be necessary to repair the damage done and restore a loving, and safe relationship with yourself where you agree to never betray yourself again.

If you are not ready to apologise, nothing can be done.

Now back to the five keys…

---

[28] From Martin Luther's *Explanation of the Lord's Prayer*, Sixth Petition ("And lead us not into temptation"), paragraph 161.

4. Ready to reconcile

Having worked through the complete and effective apology are you genuinely ready and willing to be friends again. Sometimes when a relationship has been strained for a significant time, it has worked for one party to lock the other out in the cold and treat them like the villain. When a full apology is offered and accepted, they still seem to want to continue the guardedness.

All is forgiven and forgotten, but that doesn't mean I'll trust you again.

Could you imagine how that would feel to treat yourself this way? It is incredibly unkind. If you are not willing to open yourself and remove all guardedness, then trust cannot be rebuilt.

If you are not ready to reconcile, nothing can be done.

5. Ready to begin again

Now that the space is clean between you and trust has been fully restored, are you ready and willing to go and play in the world knowing that you are likely to trip and fall and violate the relationship with yourself again?

Just because the space is now clean, does not guarantee it will stay that way. But are you ready to have a real relationship with yourself and clean the space again every time it gets polluted in the future?

If you are not ready to begin again, nothing can be done.

Here's how these ideas all flow together:

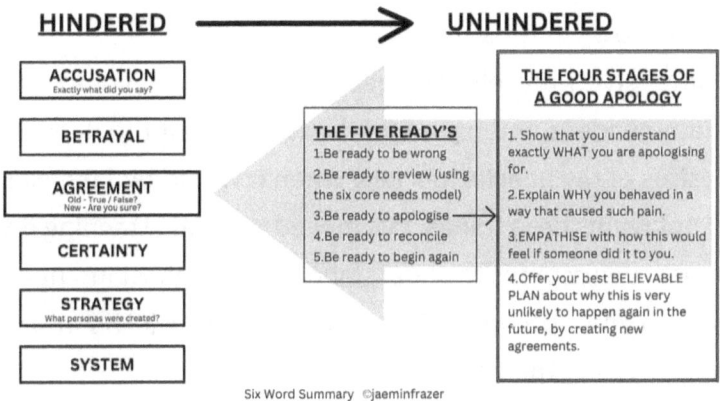

Six Word Summary ©jaeminfrazer

Trusting myself

When I consider how it is that I've turned my dreams into reality there are three principles that have been at the heart of my success.

a) I trust myself.
I know who I am. I like who I am. I have resolved the self-betrayal and woundedness of my past and have completely

restored trust within myself. There is not a moment spent managing my own behaviour for fear of what will happen if I relax. I trust my motives and intentions. I trust my natural ability to achieve the results I desire. This has created such extraordinary safety within my own relationship with myself that I am completely free to go play in the world. If I know, like, and trust myself, then what is there to fear in the world?

b) I know what I want.

I have given myself the space to explore, develop and examine ideas and have told the truth about the deepest desires of my heart especially when it would be far easier to not want these things. I've moved beyond attaching my hopes to outcomes to understanding the highest intention behind the outcome so I'm free to use or jettison any vehicle along the way.

c) I've gone all in.

Off the back of deep trust and honest desire, I've organised everything toward the most important goals. I've created these results in the unseen world, understood and accepted the price required to achieve them and readied myself to receive all that I desire as my present reality. Without the foundation of trust, there is no possibility of complete desire and wholeheartedness.

6. How to rebuild trust

Can you be trusted also? When you understand who you really are and agree that this is true, then YES of course.

7.
Safety concern number two: You keep showing up needy

In certain situations, and with certain people, you smell of neediness.

Safety breech number two follows logically on from the lack of trust raised as the first red flag. If you do not trust yourself to meet your needs, of course you must trust in someone or something else.

The outsourcing of your certainty, responsibility and direction to others is all the child can do, but the very definition of adulthood is self-sufficiency, so to continue needing others to meet your needs leaves you precariously placed. If those you rely on to fill your cup play their role, then all is well. Yet the moment they withhold your needs from you, you are instantly in deficit with no alternate fuel source.

Worse still, to be needy is to repel. It is the weakest and least attractive relational posture.

As hard as this may be to hear, the safety officer is not presenting this news to shame you or make you feel bad or wrong, it's just that neediness is very dangerous.

The good news about this operating system deficiency is that the only reason it is being brought to your attention is because there is a clear upgrade on offer.

Six Core Needs

The first time I heard of the 6 core needs it radically changed my life. I hit the jackpot at a garage sale one frosty Saturday morning when I found an unopened box set of Tony Robbins CD's for only $10. A few weeks later in my car, I heard him describe the power of his model in a way that revolutionised my thinking about my own nature and the reasons I behave in certain ways.

As mentioned in the previous chapter, Tony explains that each of us have six basic human needs that are just as essential for our survival as food, water, and shelter. The six needs come in three pairs and each pair exists in tension although they are opposites. That is to say, that both needs need to be met at the same time. Recapping the six core needs in their 'paradox pairs':

Certainty and Variety

Significance and Love

Contribution and growth

Listening to Tony explain this model on his original CD's, he taught that all needs must be met, at all times. And that we all need just as much certainty, variety, significance, love, contribution, and growth as everyone else.

Since then, however, every half-arsed, shiny life coach has butchered and diluted this model in such a way that it has made it all the way back to Robbins himself and caused him to change the way he speaks about how these needs work. Now you can take a test on Tony's website that identifies your most important needs as a function of your personality type.

This deviation from the original model now suggests that these needs exist in a hierarchy.

There is no hierarchy

Although, the clear advantage of this heresy is how well it works as a marketing funnel, the problem is that it protects, excuses, and even empowers dysfunction as simply a result of having a greater need for one or more of the core needs.

For example:

- If the test reveals your primary core need is certainty, you can be excused for being a control freak, risk averse, fearful, anxious, and therefore remain in your comfort zone.

- If your primary need is variety, you can get away with being scattered, unplanned, late, disorganised, transient, uncommitted, and rebellious. It is not your fault!

- If your primary need is significance, that explains why you are needy, selfish, narcissistic, a people pleaser, externally motivated, arrogant, egotistical, and overly driven.

- If your primary need is love, that explains why you are needy, dependant, clingy and compliant.

- If your primary need is contribution, then of course you will always need to be seen doing things for others and giving of your time, energy, and money sacrificially.

- And if growth ranks highest, that can excuse your driven-ness, restlessness, overachieving, and dissatisfaction with your current results.

While this may appear to explain why you behave in certain ways, again it does not hold up under scrutiny.

A friend of mine tried to use this logic to explain why he was risk averse, anxious, overly cautious, and analytical, and I appeared adventurous, confident, carefree, with a large appetite for risk. It made sense to him that we simply had different primary needs. He clearly needed more certainty, and I required far more variety.

The truth is, that we both need exactly the same amounts of both certainty and variety. I can't survive in the world with any less certainty than he can, it's just that I have developed a high quality, internal way of being my own certainty and so my cup is always full, whereas his strategy is all external and unresourceful and so his cup leaks. Sure, he definitely has a higher *felt* need for certainty, but that just betrays his low-quality source and how little certainty he receives from the world.

7. Safety concern number two: You keep showing up needy

To come back to the foundational idea that there is no hierarchy, means that each of us need all the core needs to be met at all times. And every behaviour is simply an attempt to meet these needs in the best way we have available to us at the time.

Without this understanding, it inevitably causes people to be highly confused about their nature, identity, and personality. (Which then undermines their willingness to trust themselves completely).

These are the most common misunderstandings that underpin the faulty assumptions about yourself:

- Your character is most accurately demonstrated by your behaviour.

- Bad behaviour proves there is a problem with your nature.

- You are what you do and so your identity is entirely connected with your performance.

- Your personality is the culmination of your patterns of behaviour.

When you take a clean look at yourself through the lens of the 6 core needs model, an entirely different truth emerges:

- You always do the best you know how with the resources available to you at the time.

- Your behaviour is simply a strategy for meeting your needs, not a reflection of your true nature.

- You are not what you do. Your identity has nothing to do with your strategy for meeting your needs and protecting your fears.

- Your personality is not the persona you've developed in a certain season to meet your needs and protect your fear. You are not your personas.

Behaviour is at the end of the assembly line in the factory of our lives and as such, every behaviour is clear evidence of the cleverly designed strategy to meet your needs externally.

The aim of the game is not to stop needing, but to meet your own needs internally. This means becoming your own source and supply.

7. *Safety concern number two: You keep showing up needy*

The transactional model

If you have not established a high quality, adult, internal strategy to meet your six core needs that are in line with your most current goals and values, then you can only be meeting these needs externally, unresourcefully, and childishly.

The child can only look outside themselves for these needs to be met simply because they do not have the internal resourcefulness required to fill their own cup. However, while the child may not have the capacity to be their own source, they instinctively know that if they don't have these needs met, they will die. They must look to the adults in their world as the most likely place to have their needs satisfied.

Without full conscious awareness, the child comes to accept that there is always a quid pro quo; a 'this for that' exchange. Unconditional love is an illusion. It's a game. I want you to give me certainty, significance, and love, so what would I have to do to get that from you?

Children are far more perceptive than they are often given credit for. They are in a crucial stage of formative sense making. – *"Oh, I see, your body language towards me when I'm emotional leaves me feeling disconnected, unloved and unsafe. When I'm stoic though, you seem to enjoy being around me much more. Got it…I'll supress my emotions and always be calm, measured and even around you, and in return you'll give me acceptance, approval and love."*

Because the child has needs and must do whatever it takes to have those needs met, they strategically must create a persona that gives them the best chance of meeting the requirements on their side of the transaction. The problem is that the created persona becomes so well rehearsed, that it confuses them and others, about who they really are.

It is likely that if no updates have been installed to your operating system you are still playing the same transactional game of meeting these needs you first established as a child.

To gain permission to move forward will require an urgent software update of your central operating system for how you meet needs. Version one of the operating system developed while you were a child is incapable of handling the demands of your adult programs. Without updating, the entire system is likely to crash. The adult upgrade is to develop an internal strategy for meeting all six core needs and to eradicate childish fears by examining and deconstructing them.

The longer you leave this update, the harder it becomes to install. The level of fear, existential angst and self-deception undermining trust and increasing neediness only intensifies.

This leads to ineffective behaviour management strategies and trying to improve your life by overriding the system rather than updating it.

Terry the recovering people pleaser

For example, Terry is trying really hard not to be a people pleaser anymore. He thinks the great challenge he is facing is that he so desperately wants people to like him, so all his best energy goes into keeping others happy. When you understand the transaction being made however, the truth becomes clear. Terry is NOT trying to get others to like him. He is trying to meet his needs for significance and love. His STRATEGY, developed as a child, is to learn how to behave in a way that coaxes nice things out of others to fill his cup. If I say yes to you, you'll tell me I'm a good person and want to be around me more often.

No matter how good Terry becomes at managing this people pleasing behaviour, it will continue to be the unconscious strategy for meeting his needs for significance and love until he finds a way to meet these needs internally.

Maybe we should leave the past behind us?

While the six core needs model provides great logic to make sense of why we do what we do, most people find it particularly difficult to analyse all their own behaviour and see these things clearly. For this reason, they seek some other way of changing their behaviour without understanding why they behave like this in the first place.

British hypnotist, behavioural scientist, and bestselling author, Paul McKenna aims to help people do just that, arguing that understanding is overrated.

In his book, *I Can Change Your Life In 7 Days*, Paul says "The myth that it takes a long time to change has only been around for about a hundred years when Freudian analysis became the dominant influence in the treatment of psychosomatic illness. What makes this point of view ironic is that psychoanalysis isn't really about changing people, it's more to do with helping them gain a deeper understanding of why they are the way they are."

McKenna claims that personal change does not require understanding at all! "In my work, understanding is the booby prize."[29] That is to say, understanding your behaviour is an embarrassing gift that no one really wants.

---

29 Change your life in 7 days. Paul McKenna. Transworld publishers, London, 2004 – P11

7. Safety concern number two: You keep showing up needy

While I agree that change happens in a moment, to imagine that fully understanding your current results is a false prize is difficult to fathom.

However, McKenna is not alone in this thinking on this subject. This same idea is propagated by hypnotherapists and NLP practitioners around the world. Their focus is entirely around creating instant change by directing powerful programming to the subconscious mind without the need to investigate any of the specifics of where the initial programming came from. This is particularly attractive to those who carry a high level of angst, shame, and trauma about the pain of their past. The major selling point is pain-free change.

> Here are tools and techniques that will alter your internal representation of a painful situation and therefore set you free from your suffering. Change your past without having to think about it? Who wouldn't want that?!

While I'm not disputing the power of hypnosis and NLP to alter subconscious patterning, my concern is that without cognitive understanding the experience can only be categorised internally as some kind of magic/mystic phenomenon. This means it forever remains supernatural to you – You have been acted upon by something or someone outside of you. If you are not in any way responsible for what happened to you, then you have no control over recreating the experience again in the future.

I've seen many people have extraordinary breakthroughs while under hypnotic trances and through the skilful use of NLP scripts, but when they come back to the everyday running of their lives, they have no structure to make sense of these changes and are no better placed to handle the next challenge coming their way. This inevitably leads them to discount the validity of their breakthrough because they don't know how to access it again or recreate it. The wonderful experience of being free from pain and suffering then gets written off as an apparition, a mirage, or a trick of the mind.

The madness of fearing understanding can only be due to remaining misdirected about the truth. When you are willing to step into the light and see the truth about your fears, full understanding is wonderful, beautiful, and extremely valuable.

Understanding is NOT the booby prize

As a teenager, I loved maths and physics. They were always my best school subjects by far and I enjoyed the logical patterns and predictable structures of these disciplines.

Throughout my life, any information that made sense to me and had a direct and immediate application became almost impossible to forget. As such, the mathematical formulas of my high school years have found a special cave in my brain that is protected from the wind and rain of time and have remained there exactly as they were installed to this day.

As a parent, I assumed my offspring would automatically share this aspect of my genetic makeup. To my dismay however, as they progressed through their schooling, I spent many painful nights trying to transfer my love of mathematics to the pair of them to no avail.

At the time of writing this book, my son is in the early stages of a carpentry apprenticeship and to his dismay, many of the mathematical formulas he managed to escape while at school have chased him down at TAFE. And now he has an urgent reason to understand them, which means he is again in need of my help.

The first subject we tackled together was geometry. Specifically, he was required to understand how to measure the volume of cylinders to calculate how much concrete would be needed to fill pier holes in the foundation of a building. At 16 years of age, I was confident that his schooling would have filled his brain with at least some of the understanding required to solve this problem but that notion vanished when he tried to repeat the stupid formula the teacher had written on the board for them.

> My son: Dad, it's TXR2. That's how you do it. That's what was on the board. You write this number in here and press this button on your calculator or something. I don't want you to explain how it works. I've already had the maths lesson, just show me what to do.
>
> Me: Yeah, but do you even understand what this formula even means?
>
> Son: Yes, dad it's TXR2! Stop trying to teach me something. Show me where these buttons are on my calculator!
>
> Me: Ok, that's not a T, it's called Pi (π). That's not an X, it's a multiplication sign. That's not a 2 it's squared (r^2), so to help you get the right answer, whether you like it or not, I have to explain what these things mean.

His whole strategy for getting the right answer was to try to remember what things to press on the calculator like the teacher did. But with zero understanding of what any of those signs meant, or what the point of the question was, he could only ever get this specific answer once. And getting it right gives him nothing useful to get any other variation of this question right. He doesn't want to understand. He just wants the quickest way to the correct answer, but without understanding, the answer is useless.

And so, the structure of how and why this formula works, and the structure of how and where this formula can be applied to get you more of what you want, is essential to understand.

I was coaching a lady who quit halfway through because it moved too far from her magic/mythic worldview. In order to serve her desired outcome of being fully free from debilitating insecurity I kept drawing her into the structure of the precise nature of the how, what, and why of insecurity. She had such an overwhelming and physical response to my coaching style that she completely shut down and explained that she literally couldn't hear another word from me on the subject.

The only way I could make sense of it, was that it was exactly the same as my son only wanting the magic formula with a huge resistance to needing to understand why the formula worked and what it actually means. This is an unnecessary tragedy. If I apologise to her for my coaching style, I also have to apologise to my son for leading him to understanding.

In our house we have a rule, stand up when you are right

and back down when you are wrong. It is very important to apologise, make amends and change your ways when you are proven to be wrong, but it is just as vital to hold your ground and fight for your cause when you are right.

To apologise when you are not wrong is to weaken the fibre of your existence. If I apologise to my client, I must stop coaching altogether. If I'm wrong about the importance of structure and the value it brings to a person desiring to improve the quality of their life, I'm wrong about absolutely everything and I must stop what I'm doing immediately.

I believe in her ability to handle the truth in the same way I believe in my son's ability, and in the exact same way I believe in my ability.

Insecurity is not built on the truth. It is a work of fiction that has gone unreviewed and has become true as a self-fulfilling prophecy does. It is impossible to consistently think new thoughts about a subject without a new framework to hang those new thoughts on.

Paul Mckenna telling you not to worry about understanding is setting you up for a lifetime of remaining stuck in your dysfunction. You may experience a short-term escape from your pain through a clever magic trick, but without understanding what, how, or why, you are locked out of lasting transformation.

Special ways of being special

Understanding that each of us must fulfill our need for significance in some way, means that if you do not take 100% ownership for your value and worth internally, and completely see your own specialness, you must find special ways to be special. And by special ways, I mean dysfunctional at best but more likely to be ugly and even destructive strategies to validate your existence.

Here are some examples:

The martyr syndrome

> *I'm special because I'm the best person I know. I would never behave as poorly as those I must put up with. I'm even more special because of the amount of shit I can tolerate and still function with a smile on my face.*

People pleasing

> *I'm special because others like me. My specialness is reflected in my ability to make others happy often by sacrificing my own happiness.*

Bullying

I'm special because I'm better than others. I'm able to accentuate my own specialness by drawing attention to the flaws of those around me.

The advice giver

I'm special because I know more than you. I'll turn every conversation into an opportunity to share my opinion and to highlight my superior knowledge and wisdom.

The overtly religious

I own the fact that there is nothing special about me, but God believes I'm special enough to rescue. I'm special in God's eyes. I now have special knowledge, a special relationship with God and a special ticket to heaven that makes me more special than those who don't.

The point is that all external strategies to make you feel significant are highly dangerous and unsustainable.

7. Safety concern number two: You keep showing up needy

A winning strategy that came crashing down

Martin was 35 when he started getting power outages in his system. Mind you, he'd been suffering greatly for more than 15 years before he ran out of gas. When he was finally willing to step into the light, he discovered his whole operating system was set up with unbelievably dangerously wiring covered by a beautiful golden façade.

This guy got kissed on the dick by a fairy! He was born with every advantage known to man: He was white, rich, tall, handsome, intelligent, sporty, funny, wealthy and…wait for it…humble as well. At any moment of his school life, everyone wanted to be like him, with him, or actually be him. He was constantly adorned with love, adoration, and celebrated just because of who he was. He was supplied with a never-ending abundance of all six core needs in exchange for just turning up to school with his hair done.

Everything about his life was instantly successful until one catastrophic day when tragedy struck. He finished school. In an instant he'd gone from being Captain Awesome to Johnny Nobody. The real world turned out to be set up very differently from the school world. Now he was just another guy competing with thousands of others no longer being rewarded for his God given advantages.

By 21 he was bald and had put on 30 kilos. He'd left home only to discover that providing for himself was much harder than drinking milk from the teat. Because nothing extra was required of him to receive all his needs being met at school, he had no idea why his needs were no longer being met now that he'd entered the real world.

By the time he was 35 he was in a real mess. He was so upset at everyone and everything for how his life had turned out. He was working a mediocre job, earning mediocre money, in a mediocre relationship, living in a mediocre part of town. He'd become captain average and had no idea why.

He was still trying to source his needs as a child by making it everyone else's responsibility to love, accept, approve, protect, and validate him. The problem is, when you need these things from the world, you must give them what they need from you in return. That's where this situation becomes incredibly dangerous.

Now back to the safety officer and the problem with neediness

Because you also decided that you couldn't be trusted to meet your needs. You had to outsource responsibility for meeting all six core needs onto someone or something else.

This dilemma then began the transactional model where you had to exchange goods and services for the fulfilment of your deepest psychological needs.

All the research about human development confirms that this all happened before you were seven, yet here you are decades later, still running the same transactions. You are not being criticised or judged by the safety officer for developing this transactional set up in the first place, nor are you being condemned for continuing to run it the way you always have. You are being challenged to see exactly how precarious this strategy is and to see the great cost involved in swapping all your best resources for other people's acceptance and approval. Your whole venture is at risk of running out of resources while you continue with this strategy. Your neediness is killing your dreams. It would be very sad to get to the end of your life and add up the cost of exchanging your energy for someone else's momentary validation.

This is a mid-life problem. You can get away with these transactions when you are younger because you have extra energy to waste. Efficiency is not necessary for survival. Yet if you are still getting your need for certainty, significance, and love by giving your best energy to make others happy when you are forty, the inefficiency of this strategy is leaving you in danger of your whole system shutting down. There is only so much you can give of yourself in exchange for what you feel you need from others. And if you are already exhausted then you have nothing left to give – which means you are about to miss out altogether.

This is exactly why you do not have permission to succeed right now, and the safety officer has demanded this conversation.

The unequivocal message from the safety officer is that you must grow up. You've worked out how to dress yourself, feed yourself and wipe your own bum, now it's time to meet your own emotional, relational, and psychological needs as well.

Your neediness is killing you and making you suffer unnecessarily. Why would you gain more energy from your unconscious to be better at being needy? It is time for the adult upgrade instead. Of course you have needs, but when you take full ownership of your role as the need meet-er you can come into the world with your cup full not needing anything from anyone.

Imagine how safe that would make your life then. If you have your own back and supply your own needs, the world is no longer dangerous.

8.
Fully becoming an adult

Two rings

When I came to terms with the implications of Robbins' core needs model, it completely changed my life.

No wonder I was so anxious and insecure, I had been looking for my needs to be filled in all the wrong places. The people I was relying on for my sense of certainty, significance and love were terrible at satisfying my thirst. To no fault of their own, they were too busy trying to meet their own needs to have any extra capacity to meet mine as well.

To continue outsourcing responsibility for what I needed, could only leave me feeling increasingly empty, alone, and unloved and confusing me about my true value and worth.

I accepted that filling my cup was actually my job. I had

worked out how to become self-sufficient physically and financially, so clearly, I had what it took to become self-sufficient emotionally, relationally, and psychologically as well.

Although I had no clear plan about how to do this for myself, the closest reference point for what it would be like to take on this role was the wedding ring on my left hand.

I can vividly remember standing at the alter as a 19 year old boy holding Katherine's hand, about to pledge my life to her. I remember thinking that these words I was saying to her were some lofty and grandiose promises, especially at my age. I had gone against the pleas of my father-in-law to wait until I was much more financially stable before taking his daughter from him. However, I also realised that what qualified me to be speaking these words was not my track record of successful past marriages but my wholehearted commitment to be Katherine's man.

I looked into her eyes and spoke from my heart. From this moment, I've got you, I've got this, I've got us. You can rest in my love for you. You won't need to look for anyone else to be by your side in this way for the rest of your life.

In one moment, everything had changed. I'm not trialling for the role of husband or on probation to see if I'm up for

8. Fully becoming an adult

the job, I'm in. With this ring, I am now her husband, and she is my wife.

This ring is still a powerful anchor to this wholehearted love I have for Katherine 25 years later.

In the same way, I decided that I wanted to wholeheartedly commit to the role of being there for myself.

The very same day I had the revelation about meeting my own core needs, I bought a ring and put it on my right hand and spoke from my heart to myself. From this moment, Jaemin I've got you, I've got this, I've got us. I knew that I couldn't point to my past track record of knowing how to meet my own needs, but that this was not required. Again, it was my wholeheartedness that qualified me.

All these years later, that ring too is still a powerful anchor of my wholehearted commitment to be there for myself.

This threshold moment, line in the sand, all-in thinking, is a central part of ending your neediness and making the adult upgrade to meet all 6 core needs yourself. Any half-heartedness, or indecisiveness will get you into strife with the safety officer. For your operating system to be deemed safe enough to handle more speed, pressure, and growth you must be sure that you are completely committed to being the adult in your own life.

Here is a comprehensive description of the typical ways adults meet their need unresourcefully, and what the adult upgrade looks like for each of the six core needs.

CORE NEED	UNRESOURCEFUL (external)	RESOURCEFUL (Internal)
CERTAINTY comfort, safety, control	Controlling others, bullying, busyness, perfectionism, risk aversion, anxiety, blame, victimhood, comfort eating, escapism, substance abuse, self-righteousness, arrogance, hoarding, remaining in unhappy situations, addiction, self-medication, self-sabotage.	Embracing uncertainty, backing yourself, internal trust, confronting dysfunction and fear, facing up to life, knowing what you want, ordering your life towards your most important goals, taking 100% responsibility, becoming the storyteller, dressing well and walking tall.

8. Fully becoming an adult

CORE NEED	UNRESOURCEFUL (external)	RESOURCEFUL (Internal)
VARIETY uncertainty, change, surprise, adventure	Substance abuse, excessive partying, starting trouble, recklessness, busyness, self-sabotage, creating drama, constant change, being an adrenaline junky, affairs, crime, being disorganised, always running late, having a messy house.	Planned adventure, life-giving rituals, cultivating creativity, making time for hobbies and holidays, trying new things, meeting new people, playing sport.
SIGNIFICANCE importance, worth, value, independence, individuality	Putting others down, judgment, lying, prove and defend, gossip, victimhood, rebellion, neediness, people pleasing, self-harming, busyness, performance, attachment to possessions or achievements, comparison, notoriety, special ways to be special, arrogance, narcissism, and co-dependency.	Taking ownership of your own significance, self-validation, self-awareness, deeply loving and accepting yourself, being the hero in your own story, re-discovering your essence, being the prize, eradicating self-limiting beliefs, creating new agreements.

CORE NEED	UNRESOURCEFUL (external)	RESOURCEFUL (Internal)
LOVE/ CONNECTION meaningful relationships	Neediness, remaining in unhealthy relationships, busyness, settling for connection, co-dependency, shallow relationships, conforming to fit in, promiscuity, people pleasing.	Self-love, re-parenting yourself, healing past wounds, training others how to treat you, aligning your life with what you deserve and desire, writing a beautiful and compelling story to live out of, cultivating high quality relationships, loving others out of the overflow of a loving relationship with yourself, living from your heart.
CONTRIBUTION give back, add value, legacy, influence	Being a workaholic, busyness, needing to be seen and recognised by others, contributing inappropriately, doing too much, all about you.	Service, love, generosity, giving without the need for reward, adding value, giving appropriately, bringing your gift to the world.

CORE NEED	UNRESOURCEFUL (external)	RESOURCEFUL (Internal)
GROWTH become, achieve, enlarge, attain, realise potential	Growth in one area that is out of proportion with all other areas, obsessions, drivenness, undirected growth, obesity, feeding resentments, allowing dysfunction to increase.	Progress, momentum, direction, improvement, character formation, knowing what you want, directed growth.

Solving the insecurity problem for good

So far, we've covered the first two of the four requirements of the safety officer before permission can be granted.

To summarise the work required to bring safety to these two areas, the lack of trust and neediness all comes back to hidden and unresolved insecurity.

The focus of my work over the last 15 years has revolved almost entirely around the subject of personal insecurity. Most people assume that because insecurity is a universal human experience, the best we can ever hope for is better management strategies. I completely disagree. I'm convinced that not only *can* the insecurity problem in our lives be solved, but we *must* solve it. Our most important adult work is to set ourselves free from the limiting beliefs of our childhood.

There are seven essential practices for overcoming insecurity as I've explained in my book *Unhindered*[30]. They fit here as a great summary of the process involved in rebuilding trust and eradicating neediness covered so far.

Here is a brief summary of each of these practices:

1. **Step into the light.** That is to name the fear – That your worst childhood accusation of yourself would be proven true and confirmed by the world.

2. **Take 100% responsibility.** That is to own the pen – Break through the misdirection of others involvement and see the precise ways you've created your own narrative. You are not the actor in the story, you are the storyteller and have always had the pen. You are the accuser and the agree-er.

3. **Stack the pain**. That is to run an accurate cost assessment for the impact of hidden or unresolved insecurity in your life – Tell the truth about how much

---

30 Unhindered. The 7 essential practices for overcoming insecurity. Jaemin Frazer and Associates 2020

8. Fully becoming an adult

it is costing you to run and hide. Only when you've had enough can you move on.

4. **Develop a compelling vision for your life.** That is to be clear about what you want – Tell the truth about what you've always wanted instead. Only when you're sure you actually want it, can you move on.

5. **Get help from someone who doesn't care about you.** That is to follow the wizard – Find the guide who knows the way and hang on tight. This is a journey into pain and fear. It gets harder before it gets easier. No one is coming to save you, but you will need the right help to find the path and become equipped to do what only you can do.

6. **Be the hero.** That is to finally face the monster – Get your day in court. Clear your name at all costs. Do the thing that you've never been able to do even if it is impossible. You will either die or come out the other side reborn. You are the hero in this story remember. When the hero does, what only the hero can do, everyone shares in the reward.

7. **Re-write the script**. That is to write a new story – Now that the fear is gone, and the old story eradicated, your job is to write a new, compelling, and empowering one

and align yourself to it until it becomes the new default narrative you are living out of.

Overcoming insecurity though rebuilding trust and ending neediness is not the main game, but when completed successfully gives you a ticket to the main game. You are now free to direct your best energy away from proving and defending yourself and into far higher levels of meaning, purpose, and contribution. You can now connect with a purpose that is bigger than you and not even about you!

Having sorted the first 2 safety concerns causing permission to be denied, you can now turn your attention to the remaining 2 red flags.

9.
Safety concern number three: Your gameplay sucks

The third safety concern is that you keep losing some or all the games you are playing. In fact, your overall gameplay requires some significant upgrades.

This makes the list of urgent areas to review before permission is granted, because you cannot afford to keep losing any longer. To continue losing the games you are playing undermines your confidence and could even lead you to believing you ARE a loser. It is time to get some wins on the board. For this to happen, you will have to review all the games you are playing; especially the ones that don't even appear to be games – marriage, work, family, money, and business.

Gamification is to apply game principles to non-game domains. The moment you come to terms with the fact that in every area of life you are indeed involved with a high-level game, it opens a world of possibilities. Then your work is to understand exactly what games you are inadvertently playing, exit the ones you no longer wish to sign up for and start playing the right games for you with very clear understanding of how the game works and the rules for how to win.

For example, if marriage/work/money/success/life are all games, then how do these games work? How do you win? What are the rules? What version of the game are you playing? Is this the version you'd like to be playing?

The best thing about the gamification metaphor is that it takes the morality out of the equation. Is the game of UNO inherently good or bad? If you are good at darts does that automatically make you a good human as well? If you can't swim fast, does that prove you are a terrible person? Of course not. They are just games, sports, hobbies, fun etc. I'm not suggesting people don't take these pursuits seriously, or that there are not high stakes involved, just that there is no clear connection between good games and good people.

To gamify life takes so much of the pressure out of the system. Rather than being overwhelmed at having to find your life mission, ultimate purpose, and your one true destiny, if it's just a game, you can choose one that suits you, that you enjoy playing, and desire to get good at. Additionally, gamification takes much of the apparent complexity out of the areas of your life where it is hard to know what you should do.

The moment the idea of a game is introduced, there are two primary questions to resolve:

1. What is the point of this game? i.e., what is winning? Is it to score the most points, the least points, be the last man standing, have the most cards, the fewest cards, tell the truth, get away with the most lies, etc.

2. What are the rules? i.e., what are the boundaries the game is played within? What are the penalties for breaking the rules? Is there a hierarchy of rules?

The order of these questions is very important. Rules make no sense until you understand the point of the game.

I've had plenty of pushback about this gamification idea from clients who have an aversion to game playing. They either believe that they don't play games at all, or they make sure that their role is to help others win the games they are playing.

> *"Oh, this doesn't apply to me…I'm like the least competitive person I know. I hate the idea of winners and losers. Can't we all just have a good experience. Why do games demand that we beat someone else to feel successful?"*

The thing is, they've just revealed the unconscious game they are already highly committed to playing. Their belief that they play no games at all is clearly not true . It's like they are playing an open misère hand in the card game 500. This is a strategy when you win the round by deliberately losing every hand. Your cards are so low that no one can underplay you and force you to win.

Winning the 'I don't play games' game is achieved by:

- Pretending it's not a game

- Always coming last

- Preferring others

- Self-sacrifice

- Being kinder, and more loving than others through your lack of competitive drive.

It is still a game though. And there is still winning and losing. Worse still, to get ahead and see your most important goals achieved is actually registered as a loss in this version of the game, so you'll feel like a bad person if any other human is possibly impacted by you getting what you want.

Why this matters

Say you've been running your own business for 10 years and what was once highly exciting is now a chore. You have to drag your sorry arse out of bed each day to show up to the work you've created for yourself. An endless sea of questions floods your mind in a way that leaves you overwhelmed and paralysed. Should you continue or give up? Diversify or double down? Prices up or down? Outsource or keep production in-house?

To gamify your situation instantly pulls you out of this spin. Now there are only two questions instead of fifty.

1. What is the point of this game you are playing?

2. What are the rules?

Once you've understood this, there are only four options for gameplay:

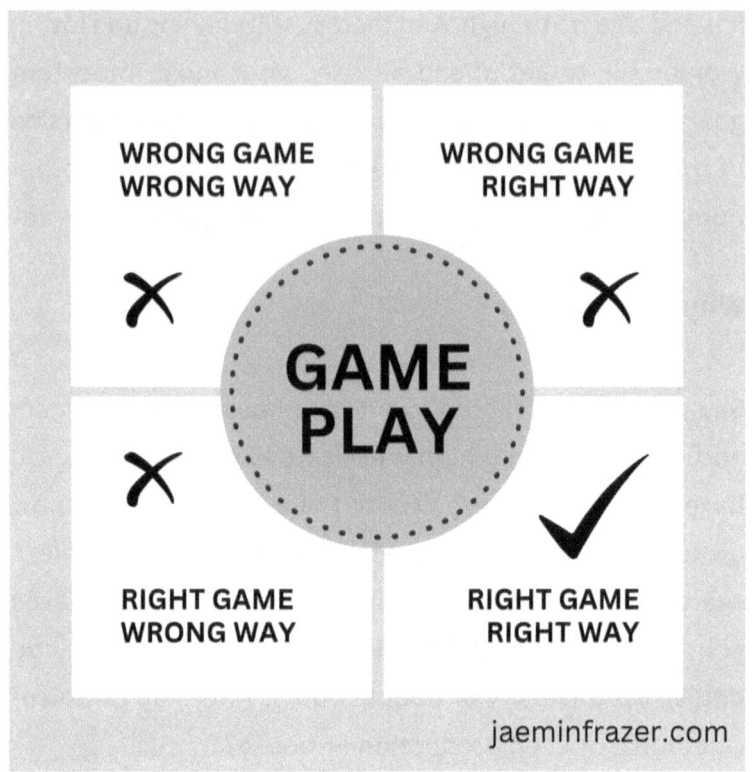

A. You are playing the wrong games the wrong way

You haven't intentionally chosen the games you find yourself playing. You don't like these games, don't have any skill, and don't desire to get better at the game. You've found yourself caught up in the games other people are playing even though you've always hated their game and have never stood a chance at winning.

Example:

- You left school without any clue about what to do with your life. Your dad suggested that being an accountant would be a good job and so you took his advice. 20 years later you are working long hours as an accountant, working your way to eventually becoming a partner in the firm, even though you hate working with numbers, you are a lousy accountant, and you suck at climbing the corporate ladder where every young upstart constantly overtakes you.

It is not hard to imagine how detrimental to your soul it would be to show up to work every day playing the wrong game the wrong way. In fact, it is not overstating the point to say that these games are sucking the very life out of you. No wonder they are a red flag safety issue.

B. You are playing the wrong games the right way

This means you didn't choose the games you are playing and are not naturally suited to them at all, but despite this, you've still found a way to win these games anyway. This dilemma is more problematic than the first one because it is far harder to break free from. Winning the wrong games becomes particularly confusing. Continuing the example from above with a slight variation, you'll see why this gets tricky.

- You hate working with numbers, and office life is boring, but you've learnt how to be an excellent accountant. Your clients always thank you for the work you do and you've also become particularly good at internal politics and climbing the corporate ladder so now you are about to become a partner and seal your fate as a career accountant.

It's still the wrong game though. It is not what you were born to do.

C. You are playing the right games the wrong way

In this variation, you have already exited the games that other people expected you to play, or the games that didn't suit you, and you've started playing new games that suit you and that you love, but you haven't found a way to win these games yet. This becomes problematic because losing all the time is confusing you about whether you made the right decision to leave the other game. Again, this means the overall experience is one of repeated loses. This is hard for morale and ultimately you understand how unsustainable it is. Here's how this may look:

- In a moment of courage and clarity, you told the partners to stick it even though everyone said you were making a huge mistake. You finally accepted the deep truth that you'd always desired to be a high school teacher and knew you'd never be happy with anything less. You went back to university and got your teaching degree and with great joy received your first school posting only 30 minutes' drive from your house. You float into your year 10 English class to discover that its full of little shits and you've got no idea how to control the room. The kids eat you alive and spit you out at the end of each day. The other teachers are all talking about you, and you feel like a complete imposter. It takes all your strength not to dissolve into a flood of tears each day and you are drinking yourself to sleep each night to escape the anxiety of this new 'dream' life you've created for yourself.

The sunk cost bias

Exiting historic games, (especially the ones you've learnt to play well) is no small thing. Working against your ability to walk away is a piece of psychology called 'The sunk cost bias.' This is a cognitive trap that makes you feel as if you should continue pouring money, time, and/or effort into a situation since you've already "sunk" so much into it already. This perceived sunk cost makes it difficult to walk away from the situation since you don't want to see your resources wasted. This is the irrational blind spot that causes us to overeat at a buffet, continue wearing shoes that are too small, or stay in relationships that have become toxic.

We are highly motivated to prove to ourselves that our past choices were right by continuing to live out of them despite new evidence suggesting this isn't the best course of action. We fail to consider that whatever time, effort, or money that we have already expended will not be recovered.

Back to our accountancy example. If you stop being an accountant now, then you've not only wasted 20 years of your life as well as your expensive university degree, but all the time, money, and energy you've devoted to being good at tax returns as well. The problem is all of this is a sunk cost. You cannot recoup any of these expenditures, so staying longer, in a game you are not enjoying, is not actually giving you any more value. Nevertheless, playing the wrong games the right way is still a major safety issue and you will not be granted permission to succeed while ever this is the nature of your gameplay.

When you do find a way to break free from these sunk costs and pursue games that are much more suited to you, this does not automatically guarantee you'll win these new games. You must learn how to play the games properly.

D. You are playing the right games the right way

The dilemma with all the preceding gameplay variations, and the reason they are on the safety officer's clipboard in the first place, is because of how dangerous they are to continue. There is no way you will gain any more resources from your unconscious to play the wrong games, or even the right games, if they are being played in the wrong way. Instead, you will continue to experience increasing levels of resistance and sabotage as a loving attempt to get you to change tact.

The only way to have permission granted, and therefore the full cooperation of your unconscious towards your goals is if you are playing the right games in the right way! Surely this is a wonderful relief to know that there is a part of you with such wisdom to demand this of you.

Practically speaking, this means you have deliberately and completely exited all games that are NOT right for you. By the time you've reached midlife you have more than enough data to analyse and reach this conclusion. If you haven't found a way to enjoy working with numbers for 20 years as an accountant by now, then it is fair to accept that you are just not a numbers person and are not suited to this game at all.

Mid-life is a time to stop experimenting and instead double down on what you already know. It is not conceited, arrogant or dangerous to close off certain options or opportunities once you've reached mid-life. In fact, it doesn't matter how you feel about keeping your options open or how proud you are of continuing to find the positives in everything when the safety officer has demanded an alternate approach. Now is the time to pick your path. Now is the time to say NO, or no more, or never again. Stop saying you can't keep doing this and actually stop doing this.

Having said NO to what you don't want, frees you to fully say YES to what you do want instead. What are the games you've always wanted to play, that you naturally gravitate towards and always enjoy?

More than just signing up to play these games, self-permission is also deeply dependant on you learning the rules. You will never have a winning experience in the games that are suited to you without a complete understanding of exactly how these games work and how to exploit all the rules to your advantage.

To be granted permission will require a proactive and crystal-clear approach to all the games you are desiring to play in the current season of your life. This includes a full understanding of the rules of the game and a willingness to learn the skills required to win the game. Without this gamification upgrade, you will continue to play all the games you are involved in poorly.

Bringing the accountancy example full circle:

- You remember how it felt to sit in the classroom with your favourite teachers when you were in high school and are reminded about the power of teaching to shape the destiny of young people and the great difference between the teachers that could control the room and those who went home crying. You reach out to the school principal to learn the rules of the game and pick up every book you can find on the art of teaching. You reset your position in the classroom and stop trying to befriend the students. After a month, teachers and students alike have noticed the difference. You are here to stay, and you are serious about being good at this. The spark in your eye has returned and the anxiety has gone. It is all going to be OK.

Timeframe and Seasons

A key feature of most games is that they have a time limit. While there are some infinite games that go on indefinitely, most games are finite. This is useful to consider when auditing your gameplay. Just because you've been playing the right game currently doesn't guarantee it will always be the right game. You've played soccer for 10 seasons with the boys, but are you going to play again next season?

As a parent, introducing the language of seasons into your game play helps to factor in the constant change in the relational dynamics you have with your kids as they grow up.

The game you'll have to play to successfully parent toddlers is very different to parenting teenagers. And if your children are still living at home in their 20's you cannot play the teenage parenting game any longer. Yes, you are still playing the parenting game, but each season will require a specific kind of parenting game within the game.

Game review questions

To get the safety officer to sign off on this upgrade you'll need to be crystal clear about some or all of these game questions:

- What is the meta game? (The main category of game)

- What is the type of game? (The subcategory name)

- What is the game within the game? (The most specific

version of the sub-category)

- What is the point of the game?
- What are the rules of this game?
- What is a foul/penalty?
- What is your motivation for playing?
- How does my game interact with other people's games?
- What time is on the clock?
- What is winning?
- What is losing?
- What is the prize?

Lebron James

I'm a huge Lebron James fan and although I was initially grieved at his decision to leave his hometown team in Cleveland to chase a championship with Miami, I quickly dried my eyes and changed team colours with him. While there was much hype about his first season playing with

Dwayne Wade and Chris Bosch in Miami, the team failed to meet expectations and they got beaten by Dallas in the finals 4-2. After his retirement, Wade revealed the key conversation he'd had with Lebron in the off season that changed their fortunes the following year.

For the preceding five seasons, the Miami Heat had been Wade's team. He was the guy. When Lebron had transferred to the Heat in the summer of 2010, he'd told Dwayne that nothing had changed in the hierarchy. It was still his team. While Lebron was arguably the biggest name in Basketball at the time and had been 'the guy' at Cleveland, he deferred to Dwayne's leadership and settled into a number two role.

The problem was that when the game was on the line, in the crucial moments the team always seemed confused about who should get the ball and make the play. LBJ is such a dominating presence on and off the court, that although he'd told everyone he was a number two, and all plays should go through Wade, he looked an awful lot like a number one.

After Miami's painful finals loss, Wade swallowed his pride and told Lebron that this was his team now. He was the guy. All plays would go through him, and he would have the ball in his hands when the game was on the line. The heat went on to win 2 out of the next 3 finals series.

9. Safety concern number three: Your gameplay sucks

Lebron was not just playing basketball, he was playing 'win a championship' basketball. For some teams, a winning season is just to make the playoffs, or even to increase the size of their supporter membership. That's not Lebron's game though. Anything other than an NBA title is a loss. There is no other game.

In 2010-11 he was playing championship ball as a number 2 which got weird, but now he got to adjust his game to be back as a number 1 again. Dwayne Wade was also playing championship basketball and came to see that his best chance of winning another ring was to play as a number 2, not a 1. Games within games within games. It all matters though.

My podcasting game

One of my mates had been hassling me about getting into the podcasting game for months despite my hesitation. I had no idea how to set up the recording gear or anything about the online requirements to host, sync, and share my content to the major platforms. One morning over coffee, he told me that I'd just have to work that stuff out because he'd just booked my first guest.

Bloody hell! Looks like I'm a podcaster now.

I managed to scramble my way to setting up all that I

needed to get my show live a week later and started advertising my podcast online. Two years later, with more than 80 episodes under my belt, I experienced a bunch of weird internal resistance to continuing my show. When I finally got to the bottom of things, it was a permission problem. I was being halted in my tracks because my set up was not safe.

The main concern from the safety officer was the way I was playing the podcast game. When I had fallen into the game two years earlier, I'd not deliberately understood or answered any of the game questions. As such, I always felt like I was losing. To release a podcast each week required a significant amount of time and energy, but I couldn't see how all that time and energy was getting me anywhere.

Without clearly defining my gameplay, the only possible outcome is that I would find myself getting caught up in someone else's version of the game. For example, the Joe Rogan game. He's the most successful podcaster, so maybe I should have more unstructured conversations with a wider range of guests, and we should smoke and drink while talking. The longer the episode, the better. Or the Tim Ferriss game. To have a wide range of interesting guests, but always ask them the same set of questions.

In other versions of the game, winning is having the best

audio, or the best graphics, or the greatest number of listeners, or the most episodes, or the most famous guests.

I realised that I felt like a podcasting loser because there was no way I could compete in any of these games. Thankfully, the more closely I examined these games, I realised I had no desire to compete on these fields anyway. I took stock of what I was doing and where I was heading and became crystal clear about my own game.

What's the point of having a podcast in the first place?

- The purpose of my podcast game is to spread a message about insecurity as a solvable problem in a way that makes it easy for people to listen to.

- Because there are very few experts in the world who consider insecurity solvable, I will only have the occasional guest on my show. This is not a platform for a variety of ideas and opinions about the subject of insecurity, the goal of this show is to help people eradicate insecurity completely. I will not have guests on the show who haven't worked through their own insecurity or who believe the best anyone can do is to just manage these human fears.

- Most of my episodes will be my own thought leadership

yet I will not add to the noise. Just putting content out for the sake of it is a major game violation. Therefore, I will only put out a new episode if I have something valuable to say. Consistency is NOT king in my game. Quality wins instead.

- I will make my episodes as short as possible, not to win the briefest episode game, but to cut out all extraneous information. Just get to the point Jaemin. I will be kind to my listeners and will never take their attention for granted.

- I am a spiritual teacher. My podcast will feel like it is touching people's whole being. To play this game well, I'll have soulful backing music quietly softening the resistance to change and touching my listeners heart in ways beautiful music only can.

- I'll make the audio as good as I can with my own basic editing software. My audio does NOT need to be perfect. Just not annoying. I do not need to waste time and money sending each episode to a professional editor or fuss over producing studio quality precision.

- My graphics will be simple, and easily produced in house as well. My artwork should look professional, but you can't listen to a podcast picture, so I won't spend extra time or money getting this perfect.

For me to satisfy the safety officer, I also had to clearly define the game time frame. Is this a game that I must play forever, or are there seasons?

Just like basketball, the clock plays a huge role in the game. Each play is restricted to a 24 second shot clock. Each quarter is stopped at 12 minutes. Each game is concluded after 4 quarters. Each season is marked with 82 regular games and then 4 rounds of playoffs.

What am I committing to? This play, quarter, game, or season?

My game is an episode-by-episode commitment. Each new podcast to be released may very well be my last. I can stop playing this game as soon as I've got nothing else to add.

When I'd finished tying down all the specifics of MY podcasting game, I got permission back. It was instantly safe to power up again because all my best energy is being directed towards a game I want to play, am good at playing and in which I can get some real wins on the board.

An echo chamber

After releasing my last book *Leverage*, I was interviewed on a podcast specifically focused on questioning authors on their latest work. A month after the episode went live, the host of the show reached out and asked if I might return the favour and interview him about his book on my show. After reading his book however, I had to decline. We were approaching similar themes about personal change but with very different solutions.

When I broke the bad news to him that I only interview guests who agree with my convictions about insecurity as a solvable problem, he warned me about the dangers of living in an echo chamber. He also suggested that a key safeguard against arrogance and insular thinking was to surround oneself with people who brought a variety of opposing viewpoints.

Because of my recent game play audit, I was completely relaxed about my decision despite his warning. I knew that's not how my game works. Most people believe insecurity is part of our flawed humanity and therefore unsolvable. This is a tragic misunderstanding and my life's work is to help people think clearly about limiting beliefs so that they can be replaced with empowering ones. What would it serve my audience to confuse them each week by having various 'experts' tell them I'm wrong about insecurity and the best they can do is to develop a range of behavior management strategies?

Rank your games

The final step to have permission granted in the game play puzzle is to rank all your 'right games' in order of importance in this season. Each game that you play has significant costs involved and it is unlikely that you'll only want to play one game well. When one of your games collides or competes with another for resources, you must know which game takes precedent in this season.

At any one point in time, it is usual to be playing multiple games simultaneously. I'm currently playing the personal development book writing game, but I'm also involved in high level marriage, parenting, friendship, farming, and business games. If I pretend I'm not married or that I have no children while I devote myself solely to writing, I may produce an outstanding book, but if I end up divorced and have my kids hate me, then winning the writing game will have ruined my life.

If you ignore the conversation with yourself about the ecology and order of your games, then expect permission to be denied.

Here are some examples of the hierarchy of my current games in this season:

Writer, speaker, coach – in that order.

My purpose comes before my relationships.[31]

Katherine and I will be good parents, but it's not the only thing we'll be good at. The empty nest game has always been in our minds eye. We will not sacrifice our marriage for the sake of our children.

Business before running. Running serves my entrepreneurial vision.

Chunk up and down

The more you gamify your life the more apparent it becomes that there are games within games within games. At times it will be important to chunk down to the most specific version of the game you are playing within the broader game. This allows you to be precise about your strategy for success and focus on your next move. Other times it is more beneficial to chunk up to the highest level of games you are playing to understand what it's all for and to gain perspective on the overarching rules governing all other games.

See what happens when you chunk all the way up to the game of life.

---

31 A direct quote from 'The way of the superior man' by David Deida. Sound true, Boulder, 1997 – p 27.

The game of life

It is super difficult to understand the game of life as a child, teenager, or young adult, but if you've made it to the mid-life season still without a clue about how the game of life works, with 100% certainty, it will be on the safety officer's list of red flag urgent operating system upgrades. Having been given a ticket to the game of life but having no idea of the rules, is significantly dangerous to your health and wellbeing.

There are plenty of ways to play this game wrong, all of them end badly for you though.

Friends star, Matthew Perry gives a very public example of this kind of poor and dangerous gameplay. His autobiography is one of the worst books I've ever read yet it is also at the top of my most recommended read list. It is such a stunning tale of the tragedy that unfolds when you misunderstand the game of life and have no willingness to learn how it works – even when the world gives you the very best it has to offer.

I have no issue with him (or anyone) telling the story of the difficult, unfortunate, or unfair things that have happened to him, but for Perry to have found no meaning in his suffering or healing for his wounds means he is still telling the story from a place of darkness. It is incredibly difficult to listen to him speak about his pain while he is still inside of it, especially while his story also includes fame, fortune, and glory all while dating some of the most glamourous sort after women in the world.

He is a lonely, bitter, sad old man, still angry at God, the world, and his mother. Still very much a victim of his circumstances and still getting his ass kicked by the game of life.[32]

The five rules of the game of life

The introduction in Napoleon Hill's book, *Think and Grow Rich,* is perhaps the greatest book introduction in the history of writing. He says that the secret to wealth is contained in this book no less than 100 times. However, not once is it written explicitly. You will have to look for it. You will only find it if your heart is open, and you are ready to receive. The secret is there as plain as day for anyone that wants to understand it. He just can't tell you directly what that secret is.

Brilliant.

You must lean in, otherwise, you'll miss it. Even though it is right in front of you, if you do not interact with the truth, you can't have it.

---

32   Matthew Perry tragically passed away from an accidental ketamine overdose shortly after I wrote these words.

9. Safety concern number three: Your gameplay sucks

In a similar way, explaining the rules of life in five simple sentences may do you a disservice. Just like the secret of wealth, you can only understand when you are ready. Without readiness, these rules are easily dismissed and discarded as useless.

Nevertheless, much has been written by spiritual teachers throughout the ages about the game of life and there is a rich vein of shared wisdom to draw from in understanding the rules. Let me attempt to give you a taste of how the game works.

Let's refer back to the two central game play questions to begin:

a. What is the point of the game?

Winning the game of life = Genuine happiness, fulfillment, purpose, peace, contentment, satisfaction, joy, love, finding yourself, reaching potential, congruence with values, meaning, transcendence.

Losing the game of life = remaining lost, stuck, needy, anxious, lonely, separated, insecure to the point of madness.

b.   What are the rules of the game?

1.   Life is unfair.

2.   The obstacle is the way.

3.   Desire beats deserve.

4.   All we have is story.

5.   Everything is spiritual.

Like I said, easy to miss or dismiss. Let me add a little more depth to each of the rules.

1.   Life is unfair.

Oh, you thought that when things became unfair, you were entitled to feel sorry for yourself and complain to others that you deserved a better deal. No, I'm really sorry, but that is not how this game works. Who told you that it was supposed to be fair? Open your eyes and look around. There is great inequality and injustice everywhere, and there always will be. Life IS unfair. That is not a glitch in the game, that IS the game.

While it is objectively true that life is unfair, you will have

9. Safety concern number three: Your gameplay sucks

abundant opportunities to feel justified in complaining about your situation and playing the victim card. No one could blame you for this or say that you should not be upset. You are entirely correct. It is unfair. You have been dealt misfortune. You did deserve better. You are completely entitled to play the victim card but it's a trick. The moment you do, you must sit on the bench, and you lose the game.

2. The obstacle is the way.

What looks like the impossible impediment to your progress is in fact the exact and only path to your success. It is in overcoming the obstacle, not circumnavigating it, that you are transformed.

Oh, you thought the immovable obstacle impeding your progress was the end of the game and everyone would understand why it was impossible for you to move forward and that it was entirely out of your control? No, that obstacle IS the way.[33] That's the game. What appears to impede the path IS the path.

Everything changes the moment you realise that life doesn't happen to you, it happens for you. It all belongs.

---

[33] It was Roman emperor and stoic philosopher Marcus Aurelius who first introduced this wisdom.

The misunderstanding of this rule, however, is that self-discipline is essential because you have to break through the obstacles in front of you.

3. Life rewards desire.

If you want to, you can. Even when there is no way forward and the obstacles blocking your progress are impossible to move if you want to move forward you can. You must do what is impossible. The only way forward is through the immutable power of desire.

Every day, humans do something that was completely impossible the day before. Necessity is the mother of invention. Life only responds to will. And it takes will. Go all in. Unwavering faith and extraordinary action[34]. What do you want, and what are you prepared to do about it, are the two most powerful questions in the game of life. You can be anyone you want to be.

Just like the tree growing through the crack in the rock where it seems completely impossible to do so: Oh...You want to grow here anyway. Ok you can.

---

[34] This is the Miracle Equation as described by Hal Elrod in his book by this name.

4. All we have is story.

Everything is created twice – It's all story and you have the pen. Everything has a first creation in the unseen world, either by design or by default, and then the second creation is simply the physical manifestation of what had already been created.[35] If you want it, you must first create it. See it, believe it, and prepare to receive it. Embody what you want before it has arrived in the physical form. (See the Be Do Have model in the final section of the book)

Nothing has meaning except the meaning we give it. The universe does not owe us a meaning. Therefore, we get to decide the meaning of life.

This means you and I are not real. We are a construct. We are a work of fiction. We are merely a story about the life housed in our mortal body and what it means to be us.

5. Everything is spiritual.

You'll have to work out how to be a good human first, then you can include and transcend your humanity into a universal spirituality. As a species, humans have evolved to have consciousness as part of their basic makeup. We've

---

[35] This wisdom comes from Stephen Covey and is explained in his best-selling book "The 7 habits of highly effective people"

become sense making creatures, meaning seekers and story tellers, and cannot survive without a story to live out of. This means our brains have developed the ability to be aware of our own individual existence. We can think about our existence rather than just merely existing.

Every human is born with individual consciousness – An awareness of me, or I. We have the capacity to develop a collective consciousness – An awareness of us. And, in rare but breathtaking ways, we can even transcend these levels of awareness into a cosmic consciousness – I am not me. I am that I am. I am energy, electricity, matter, life, intention. I am the cosmos. I am god.

Psychedelics are part of the grace provided for us to understand and experience this element of the game. Of the most common shared revelations of a hero dose of psylocibin is that the self dissolves. You are not there. You are not you. 'You' is a construct.

Be human before being spiritual. Those who seek a truly fulfilling and meaningful existence must take responsibility for becoming a good human first. Being able to access higher realms of consciousness and spiritual life comes as a result of including and transcending your humanity. Spirituality is central to a rich life experience, but you cannot find this by rejecting or bypassing your humanity.

It must be included. You have to work out how to be a good human before you can work on being spiritual. And that order is very important.

If your spirituality is an attempt to escape the central dilemma of your humanity, it becomes weird and toxic, and gives no value to your everyday existence.

Your games

Back to the safety officer asking for a complete gameplay audit.

Clearly, there is a bit of work involved in reviewing and reconstructing all the games you are involved in, but it doesn't really matter how hard this is when the safety officer has shut down your whole operating system and removed permission to succeed because of the dangers to your current set up.

No matter how long it takes to effectively gamify your life, you will never once regret getting this right. The full release of motivation, energy, and confidence that comes when you are playing the right games in the right way is stunning. Especially when you may have been so confused about what was wrong with you all this time.

Order of operations

The reason that game play comes in third on the list of conditions to satisfy is that you must take care of trust and neediness first. Being insecure locks you out of playing the right games in the right way.

Eradicating all insecurity from your life is your most important adult work, and yet it is not the main game. Being secure is the ticket to the main game. You are now free to direct your best energy to bigger, better, more beautiful, and more meaningful games.

Objectively, secure people play better games than insecure people. Secure people also play safer and more sustainable games in which more people benefit from because they are no longer just proving and defending themselves. They have energy to give into growth, adventure, and contribution.

To play the right games, the right way you must completely trust yourself and have developed adult resourcefulness. If you don't trust yourself, how are you supposed to know what the right games are let alone the right way to play them?

When you trust your own nature and can completely relax into your own natural ability, then the right games become which ever games you desire to play. You are free to answer the adult question honestly – What do you want?

10.
Safety concern number four: An incongruent avatar

Even when you are playing the right games, you often show up like you don't belong in the game.

The final safety breach is that you have not intentionally aligned your most important games with a winning avatar.

The word Avatar comes from the Hindu culture and means the embodiment of a persona or ideal. Once you are clear about the games you actively desire to play, then you must develop the persona who is capable of playing these games to win.

The reason it is on the safety officer's clipboard is that your current personas are incongruent with the games you are playing. It's like you keep showing up to play basketball wearing your netball skirt. It is a major safety breach to undermine your winning strategy having done all the work of upgrading the games you are playing, to then not have your game uniform on. How are you supposed to win if no one is taking you seriously, least of all yourself? To satisfy the final requirement of the safety officer, you must show up like you are the person who is ready to win the game. Take yourself seriously. Embody the persona of a proven winner.

Once you choose the right game, you must go all-in and play the game properly. This means showing up to the game like you belong and are ready to win. This may seem obvious, but I can assure you that many people get blocked at this final stage.

My daughter recently convinced her mother and I to pay half the fees of an expensive online course aimed at teaching her how to train horses in a holistic and connected way.

I watched the opening video with her, heard the trainer explain in depth how she was a lifelong learner, that she wasn't claiming to know everything about this subject she was about to teach on, and that she was inviting her participants to be students with her as they learnt together. Wait…So you're still a student? Bummer. I thought we were paying a premium for an expert!

10. Safety concern number four: An incongruent avatar

No one wants a know-all, or someone who is arrogant and conceited about the correctness of their own worldview, but if you pay top dollar for the world's best trainer, you'd hope that an expert trainer would show up to deliver the said training as a teacher not a student.

It is false humility and a dangerous play to tell people who've bought into your expert status that you are going to be students together. You are getting paid for what you do know not what you don't. Better to show up as a teacher and know what you know with precision and confidence.

Be Do Have

I still remember the very first time I thought about being the best coach in Australia. When I moved beyond feeling like a major wanker for even saying this aloud to myself, I realised that it was indeed what I wanted. If this desire was pure and based on who I was meant to be then who would it serve if I played it safe and small instead of going after this dream wholeheartedly. It's not like I wanted to play quarterback for the New England Patriots or beat Elliod Kipchoge at the marathon. What I wanted was to be excellent at the thing that is most aligned to how I'm wired and where I could add the most value. Someone has to lead the way, why couldn't it be me?

Once I'd examined my own motives for wanting this and dealt with all the limiting beliefs that said I couldn't have it, I firmly set my sights on living out this lofty goal. I understood that the only path to success was to live the BE DO HAVE model.

I've referenced this brilliant model in both *Elegantly Simple Solutions to Complex People Problems,* and *Unhindered*, so I won't labour the point again. But it does belong here though, as this is the only way to develop enough internal safety to gain complete permission to succeed. Without embodying a winner, it is impossible to win. If it is impossible to win, gaining access to full motivation is an exercise in madness.

Here is a summary of the three ways you can organise yourself within this model here:

The victim – Have, Do, Be: When I have the right stuff, then I'll do the right things and then I'll be happy and successful. The problem is that I NEVER have what I need to get started, and so I'm always waiting and comparing myself to others and never get around to doing anything.

The Worker – Do Have Be: The more I do, the more I'll have, then the happier and more successful I'll be. The problem is the more I do, the more there is still do to, and the more

I have the more there is to lose. I get stuck in this cycle of doing and having, and the being always seems out of reach.

The Winner – Be Do Have: Beginning with the end in mind, BE the exact person who has access to these results, and then as you DO everything that person would, in the way they would do them, you will HAVE what they have, and what you desire.

Rather than living like a victim, constantly waiting for the right conditions, and comparing myself to others; or living like the worker, always hustling, striving, forcing more and more each day; I followed the path of the winner.

I began with the end in mind and went ahead and embodied this person I was aiming to become, here and now already.

From the moment I set my sights on this ambition of being the best life coach in Australia, I talked to myself, and about myself, as though this was already true – before I had any right to. I got dressed in the morning like this was true, I ate my breakfast as though this was already true. I conducted every coaching session from the inward reality that this was already true. This is not 'fake it till you make it' – this is Stephen Covey's universal law that everything is created twice. The only reason others are saying this about me now is because I said this about myself first, and then wholeheartedly aligned myself to this vision every day for the last 12 years.

BEING always precedes DOING. This is the way of the winner.

What games do you want to play and who do you need to be to win them?

We can summarise and consolidate this part in the process with two questions.

1. What do you want?

After fully exploring the highest intention behind the outcome (knowing it is never about the thing you want, but what that thing represents) and all the consequences of pursuing and achieving this outcome, restate your desired outcome in a well-formed way.

2. Who do you need to BE to achieve it?

Once you are explicitly clear about what you want and why you want it, the game changing question is not 'what do I need to do?' but 'who do I need to be?' Another way of asking this question is 'what kind of a person would have access to these outcomes?' Then, your job is to simply show up embodying this person at the right time in the right way.

Who is at your table?

My other favourite way of thinking about who you want to be, is to use the "Who is at your table" model taught to me by Greg Bellingham. Imagine sitting at a conference table where you have invited all the different versions of yourself to be present and have a voice.

You may feel like there is only one of you, however a simple review of the past seasons, roles, and relationships of your life will reveal that you have shown up in a wide variety of ways throughout your life and as such, there are still multiple versions of you.

When using the 'who is at your table?' exercise, there are three things to consider.

1. Awareness of current characters

To gain a clear picture of all the past and present characters inside you, start with observing the dominant patterns of behaviour in different times, places, and roles in your life. You can then describe that behaviour by giving it a character name to identify who that character is like. You may already have clearly differentiated characters in your life identified by the nicknames you have collected over the years in different circles you've travelled.

You may also notice that you are a different person depending on who you are talking with or the role you are enacting. The point is, you already have a range of different ways of being you. Each of these personas has a set of characteristics that perform differently than the others.

2. Integration of the characters into your current game

Take note of the various decision styles each of your characters might display. Some of them work well and are resourceful, while others are unexamined and therefore offer unresourceful strategies.

All of the characters have a positive intention and so the aim is to understand and accept them rather than to judge and squash them. This allows you to utilise the strengths of each character when you need them most. You can't kill the characters. They are part of you and have helped you to get where you are today.

If you are clear about all the characters at your table and how they function, you can deliberately be the certain version of you most likely to achieve the result you desire on purpose.

3. Invitation of new characters

You created all the other characters for a purpose in a particular season, so you can also create new ones who are capable of taking you to the next chapter of the journey as well. If none of your past and present characters know how to win your current games and achieve your most important goals, then it is time to invite a new character to the table by modelling a winner.

You can give this new character a name and then create physical anchors that allow you to step into this persona wholeheartedly.

You can gamify it with these questions:

What is the character's name?	How do they operate?	What are they trying to achieve?	What are their strengths and weaknesses?	What are the rituals / anchors to access them?

And then also like this:

Role	Goal	Current Character	Ideal Character	Anchor

A wardrobe full of avatars

Winning is safer than losing. It guarantees your survival in the game. To continue losing depletes your resources and ultimately leads you to stop playing altogether.

Physical anchors are one of the most effective ways into different personas as they provide a sensual link into a different way of being. Each game requires the right avatar, and each avatar looks and feels distinct. When I walk into my wardrobe, each item of clothing is linked to a different version of myself. This is super useful to realise and build upon when updating from discipline to permission.

A distinct uniform signals to yourself, and the world, who you are being, and the game you are playing. Sometimes it works best to clearly demonstrate exactly who you are being to the world with a very well understood and precise uniform, other times it is best to be far more subtle with the main aim to signal to yourself, but not necessarily reveal your game to those around you.

There are some games where every item of clothing matters immensely, and other games where you can dress any way you like. In the latter versions, it is perhaps more important to have developed the exact persona and the anchors into this way of being, so that you know your game face is still on even when others don't.

For example, if I'm taking myself seriously as a keynote speaker, every item of clothing matters immensely, because of the huge role the crowd plays in my ability to win the game. Until I am world famous, I must look like a speaker to be invited into the collective speaking game.

Yet when I'm playing the writing game, it's just me and my laptop. The crowd doesn't play a role, so I don't require their permission for me to keep playing the game based on whether I look the part.

I still absolutely require a writing avatar and therefore must have physical indicators of the difference between this character at my table and all the others, so when I'm writing, I wear plain clothes and slip-on a chakra bracelet to my left wrist to instantly drop into writing mode. The writer is the only guy in my team who eats vegemite toast and drinks instant coffee.

Multiple games at the same time

It is important to realise that a successful life comprises of multiple winning games. If I can only work out who I need to be as a writer so that I can win the game, but then suck at the games of marriage, parenting, business, friendship, and finance, then all wins gained as a writer end up soured by the losses in every other game. You'll need clear avatars for each game, and therefore clear uniforms for each avatar. Your wardrobe matters.

11.
Permission granted

In the context of all four safety concerns, your job is to update your system so that you:

- Trust your natural ability without having to manage yourself.

- Meet all core needs yourself so that you aren't trapped in a transactional model that leaves you precariously placed.

- Exit games that you don't want to keep playing and start playing the games that work for you.

- Know exactly who you need to be in each game, in order to win and have a clear anchor or access point into each avatar.

While many people believe that it takes time to change, and trust is rebuilt slowly, you'll notice that each of these four conditions only have a binary position which means that there is no room for grey. You can't hedge your bets and have a little from column A and a little from column B. Each condition requires wholeheartedness.

These questions can only be answered one way or the other:

- Do you trust yourself fully? Yes, or no?

- Where are you sourcing your needs? Internally or externally?

- Have you exited the wrong games, started the right games, and learnt the bloody rules? Yes, or no?

- Have you developed and embodied the character capable of winning the right games you are playing? And are you able to access this avatar at the right time? Yes, or no?

Once all four conditions have been satisfied to the standard of the safety officer, the only possible experience is that permission is granted. You are free to succeed in the games you desire to play because your success is now safe.

Permission to play

When I first developed this model, performance and success was all I had in mind. I was aiming to help ambitious midlifer's who were accustomed to performing at a high level in the past but now feel strangely restricted and unable to access motivation, energy, and clarity.

Unequivocally, satisfying the four conditions of the safety officer brings performance back online, yet what I've also come to discover is that you do not only have full permission to succeed, but also have **full permission to play**.

Play belongs

Success is important, but the ability to play is even more valuable to the human experience. When you create great internal safety by upgrading your operating system there is no longer anything dangerous outside you that would warrant playing safe and small as a protection strategy. Sure, go hard at your most important goals, but don't miss the wonder of life that is now available to you through play. Have fun, laugh, cry, explore, experiment, taste, see, dream, dance, rise, fall. Swing away. Whatever happens next, you'll be OK.

You can trust your nature. You don't need anything from anyone. You understand the game of life and have bought yourself a ticket to play by eradicating all insecurity. What could be more appropriate than to use this freedom to have some fun.

12.
The Pressure Test

Fear of falling back into old habits

The fear of falling back into old habits is high on the list of concerns of almost everyone I've worked with on this upgrade. Yet this language is imprecise and unhelpful. Your unconscious safety officer will roll it's eyes every time you say or think this.

If you've renegotiated terms with yourself off the back of accepting that the central issue in your life is that you do not and will not have permission to succeed under the current set up, then once you've updated the system and gained permission, why would you want to go back to the old system? That makes no sense. There is no logic that could support that decision. In this light it is impossible to fall back into old habits.

Agreements are binary. To agree with something means you must disagree with all else. You cannot hedge your bets. You must choose what it is that is true and then agree with your own assessment.

Your past mistrust and neediness is built solely on your iron clad agreement that there is a problem with you. You can't have it both ways. If you've conducted a thorough review of the data and the past misunderstanding is clear, then to continue managing yourself as though the problem is still real is a major foul.

You are not fragile. You do not need to go softly, gently, cautiously into the world in case this new freedom is short lived. If you are trustworthy, then bloody well trust yourself. All else is completely inappropriate and a form of further self-betrayal.

Change may take a long time coming, but it always happens in a moment. We are always motivated to do the best we can with the resources we have. Once we have a genuinely better option that consistently gets better results, then the old set up gets displaced for good. Why would anyone want to revert to the old operating system if the new one is objectively better in every way?

12. The Pressure Test

The new system must be able to handle heat

What appears to be falling into old habits, is more likely to be a system pressure test.

It's great that a newly designed engine can idle in the car park, but can it handle some heat through it out on the open road?

The only way to find out, is of course to put it to the test.

If a hose breaks, or clamp comes lose, the whole engine will no longer work. This is vital feedback in fine tuning the componentry rather than a reason to define the engine as a failure and destroy the whole project.

It is one thing to be able to agree that you are worthy, wonderful and good in the safety of your own private journal, but can your agreement handle the real-world heat? What happens the next time someone behaves towards you in a way that doesn't seem to reflect your updated beliefs? Will you betray yourself again or are you still sure of who you are even under pressure?

Your system must be pressure tested like this to see where the cracks are. If and when a crack is found, there is no failure only feedback. You have not fallen back into old habits; you have just discovered the weak point in your new system. This means you know where to focus your attention to strengthen that point so that it can hold up under more heat and pressure next time.

Permission denied again

Once self-permission has been granted, all future experiences of internal resistance, self-sabotage, loss of motivation or clarity can only be due to a new breach in one or more of these four areas. This is the best practice for human motivation pure and simple.

New agreements, new standards, new rules. Broken rapport with a strong signal will only be one of these four safety breeches again.

> *Hey! You're managing me again. What don't you trust about my natural ability to achieve the result you want?*

> *Hey! You're being needy again. You are exchanging valuable resources for validation, affirmation, acceptance, love, certainty, or permission from others.*

> *Hey! You've got caught up in someone else's game again.*

12. The Pressure Test

Hey! You're not showing up like you are ready to win the games you are playing. You are confusing yourself and others.

Signal on

Because you've created a clean space within your relationship with yourself, you've now set a new precedent for how things must be from here on.

You will now have a real-time 'tell' the moment rapport is broken. You can't have a verbal conversation with yourself when this happens, so your unconscious will use physical pain as an instant signal that things are not right.

In her book, *You can heal your life,* Louise Hay teaches that problems within your body are almost always the physical manifestation of internal discord. To heal the body then simply requires you to resolve the internal issue. The problem with her theory is that she oversimplifies the connection between the physical symptom and the connecting internal issue.

If I've polluted the space between my wife and I with some misdemeanour and I can tell she is unhappy with me, it would be foolish (and dangerous) of me to guess exactly why she's upset and what I need to do to make things right.

It turns out the smart thing to do is just ask her. Then she can tell me in no uncertain terms what is wrong.

To dominate the conversation with yourself by assuming that Hay's simple cause and effect examples are the final word on the subject is bound to be met with internal eye rolling and great frustration.

Here are some of her prescribed mind/body connections: [36]

- Lower Back Pain = Fear of money or lack of financial support

- Foot Problems = Fear of the future and of not stepping forward in life

- Sciatica = Being hypocritical. Fear of money and of the future

- Snoring: Stubborn refusal to let go of old patterns

- Thrush: Anger over making the wrong decisions

Really? That's it?

---

[36] Her full list can be found here: https://theflowguy.com/louise-hay-list-of-symptoms/

12. The Pressure Test

That's what it MUST be about?

My advice is: don't guess, just ask: What is this signal for?

When I break rapport with myself, I'm instantly notified by my piriformis muscle which squeezes the sciatic nerve resulting in shooting pain down my left leg. When this first happened, I assumed it was a running injury, yet as soon as I reviewed the experience objectively, I realised I run all the time and I knew I had not done anything unusual to cause this pain. It was simply to get my attention by taking running off the table. This is a smart play because I love to run so much. I could probably live with pain in my elbow for some time because it wouldn't stop me doing anything I love, but to not be able to run! I can't cope with that.

Just like with my wife, the signal is the same every time. If I'm attentive, there is an instant indicator of broken rapport. Of course, I can pretend not to notice it, or judge her for being too sensitive, but there is no mistaking the distance that is now between us that doesn't just fix itself if left alone. There is a conversation or more likely, conversations to be had to make things right again.

Similarly, if you are serious about building an adult relationship with yourself, there will be an unmistakable pain signal within, to grab your attention and demand a conversation. You'll know you've got it right when the pain signal instantly stops. No guess work needed.

To maintain permission requires an adult relationship with yourself. Nothing less will work.

Broken rapport with self

Here is an example of a conversation I've had with my safety officer about all four conditions being broken.

My conversations with friends and family on the subject, leads me to believe that I dream at night more than the average person. In fact, I'm not sure how it would be possible for anyone to dream more than I do. It seems that dreams take over my senses for the whole time I'm asleep each night and I often wake up exhausted from the epic journey or crazy battles I've been involved in while my head rests on the pillow.

All that to say, I'm certainly not inclined to find meaning in every dream I have. To decode the vast number of metaphors and narratives I'm presented with each night would take more time than I have each day. However, occasionally there are dreams I cannot ignore. When a dream starts repeating itself over a period of weeks, or even months, it seems obvious that my subconscious has a message for me, but more than being excited to understand what that message may be, I just want the dream to stop!

The no pants dream

One such repeated pattern is the no pants dream. While the context may vary, the theme is always the same. I start the experience feeling excited and fully prepared to face whatever is in front of me, but then at some point I'm terribly embarrassed to discover that I'm not as well prepared as I thought because I've forgotten to get dressed. The moment I realise I have no pants on, a wave of dread and embarrassment washes over me, and the rest of the dream is about painstakingly trying to make it home again without anyone seeing me with my pants down.

These dreams leave me traumatized and undermine my confidence for hours when I wake. Finding a meaning then is not an exercise in abstract theorising, but in practical problem solving. This dream pattern must stop. My hypothesis is that the only reason it is on repeat, is that it carries an important message for my conscious mind. Therefore, as soon as I get the message and apply the instruction, the purpose of the dream has been fulfilled and doesn't need to happen again.

I find dream interpretation best done pragmatically. Asking Google or Siri what certain dreams mean is like asking your German friend to translate Spanish. How are they supposed to know what is being said. That's not their language. Your dreams are encoded using the unique data of your personal experience of life. Only you will ever know what you are saying to yourself.

Of course, there can be value in others listening to that data and helping you process the codified patterns of meaning, but ultimately if a dream is on repeat, your unconscious is hell bent on telling you something. The best way to find out what that thing is, is to simply ask. You will know with precision that you've accurately understood the message only when the dream stops repeating. Until then, keep listening.

Now before you start complaining about how frustrated you are because you ARE listening and you are still NOT getting the message, it is useful to remember the only thing that could possibly prevent understanding happening is a lack of willingness to receive it. If you want to understand, you can. There is no other way of thinking about it.

To be still in the dark about a pattern of dreams therefore means part of you does not want to know what they are about. You are afraid of what will be required of you if you were to get the message loud and clear. Pleading ignorant is your only valid defense.

> 'Hey, I didn't receive the message so, I can't be held accountable for not doing what you wanted!'

As soon as I was ready to stop and listen, the no pants message was loud and clear:

> Hey Jaemin, you are still showing up like the boy all the time. You keep deferring to others' wisdom, imagining that you are probably wrong and pretending not to know the things you are certain about. What's up with that? You're not the student anymore, you're the teacher. Know what you know. Stand up and speak what you believe clearly and confidently so that other people can understand you and benefit from your wisdom. You are in the certainty business. If you are not certain about what you think about subjects you've devoted your life to thinking about, how do you expect anyone else to be?

Why Mark Manson is wrong

In his bestselling book *The Subtle Art of Not Giving a F*Ck*, Mark Manson says that we are wrong about everything. "But perhaps the answer is to trust yourself less. Afterall, if our hearts and minds are so unreliable, maybe we should be questioning our own intentions and motivations more. If we're all wrong, all the time, then isn't self-skepticism and the rigorous challenging of our own beliefs and assumptions the only logical route to progress?"[37]

Well, if we are wrong about everything, I think this is one of the things Mark Manson is wrong about. It just doesn't make any sense.

The no pants dream happens when I pretend to be wrong about the things I'm right about. This message had immediate implications applications for me. It doesn't serve anyone for me to assume I'm wrong and that someone else has probably got a better way of thinking about this problem. This is the one subject I've devoted my entire life to, so you'd hope I'd reached some conclusions and was certain about my theory by now.

For this reason, I get my arse kicked and my pants get removed in my dreams whenever I show up uncertain. This means in this season; I'm not needing to learn anything else about insecurity. I don't read books or listen to podcasts on this subject. I don't ask for advice or deconstruct my models. I show up being right. Then my pants stay on, and everybody is happy.

---

[37] Manson, Mark. The Subtle art of not giving a f*ck. P 131

12. The Pressure Test

My word for 2023 was unapologetic. Believe me, that is not my normal modus operandi. I'm normally very apologetic! I'd hate to come across arrogant, conceited or closed minded. Yet what is the point of being on the backfoot just so I don't come across this way, when I'm prioritizing rapport with others at the expense of rapport with myself. It is unsustainable and unkind.

I can trust my nature, my intentions, my wisdom, my heart. It's ok to be me. There is nothing to prove or defend. I'm not wrong about that so there is no point being anything other than certain.

As soon as I came to terms with this, doubled down on what I'm certain about and showed up like the teacher and not the student, the no pants dream instantly stopped. It is important to state that while I'm closed to learning about insecurity in this season, I'm still very open to learning, experimenting, and being wrong in other areas. Currently I'm very much enjoying my learning phase in geology, astronomy, geopolitics, golf, and concreting.

The game I'm playing is facilitating transformation, and the congruent avatar to win this game is a spiritual teacher. For that, I must be certain.

Some examples of how this works

Mia is forty, and a single mother of two. She was married for fifteen years but has been divorced for three years now, and feels ready to date again, but every time she dips a toe in the dating pool, she has such a strong physical response that she immediately backs out.

When reviewing the data herself she couldn't put her finger on why dating felt so icky. She is emotionally intelligent, has lots of girlfriends, has done a lot of healing work around the breakup of her marriage, has no trouble creating great rapport with happily married men at work or the gym, and is never awkward around them. It just gets weird the moment someone is actually available, and or, interested in her. She is lonely and does want a partner to be able to share her life with, but because of how messy and painful the dating experience is, she's almost convinced herself that she's just happy being a single mum.

There is nothing broken in this system. All that Mia is experiencing is the express lack of permission from her unconscious to enter a romantic relationship. Under the current set up, dating is simply not safe. More precisely it is the single biggest threat to her future health and happiness. The misunderstanding is that she will just have to fight against her fears and misgivings brought about through

12. The Pressure Test

the painful experiences of past relationships gone bad, and just tell herself that this is different and forge on for the sake of her love life.

Have a look at what we discovered when we applied the self-permission method instead.

Reviewing the data of her childhood, Mia had to go back to the meaning she placed on being born into a home with a distant and unemotional father.

> *If the first man, and the one with the most biological, relational, and emotional reason to love her wholeheartedly couldn't or wouldn't, then clearly there is a big problem with me, and I should not expect any man will ever find enough reason to love me completely.*

From that point, a strategy must be developed to handle the fall out. So, she becomes submissive, subservient, gentle, quiet, agreeable and make every effort to please men so that they will enjoy being around her and may even enjoy it enough to become romantically involved.

> *I can't expect to just be loved. I must earn love. I must perform for love. I must give people what they need from me to receive their love in return.*

This led to a fantasy about the diamond wedding ring being the proof of value and lovability.

> *When I have a ring, I'll be able to show myself and others that I am loveable. I'll do whatever it takes to get the ring.*

Good luck with that. When the unconscious mind is withholding permission, it will also resist, sabotage and thwart all conscious plans towards the unsafe goals.

The wonderful discovery for Mia however, was that her unconscious is not her enemy and is just as committed to a happy love life as she is consciously. It just has to be safe.

To be able to truly fall in love, the central question then becomes: What conditions would have to be satisfied to make romantic relationship safe again?

The answer is the same for everyone.

Restore trust, end neediness, update the games, and show up as a winner.

Back to Stuart's story

Guess what? There were four safety concerns that required urgent attention. His unconscious mind had organised

12. The Pressure Test

strategic strike action until such time as the set up was made safe again.

Here's what we discovered:

1. Trust – He moved around a lot as a kid, never fitted in at school, got bullied badly. Accused himself of being a loser. Developed a way to be a winner in business in his adult life, but the deep betrayal and the fear of who he really is, still taunts him.

2. Needs – Because of the underlying fear of being a born loser, all his best energy was being directed into proving and defending himself so that no-one would ever imagine this was true. This left him needy for external validation, approval, and applause. The problem was that even when he got what he needed from others, it was always fleeting and only satisfied the needs momentarily.

3. Gamification – In order to be a winner in business, there are a bunch of games he felt compelled to play, none of which he enjoyed. Additionally, he'd bought into David Goggin's game of health and fitness, his business partner's game of business growth and his parent's game of marriage. To gain permission to bring his true genius to the world would require stepping

into the games he was best placed to win and had a natural ease in playing.

4. Avatar – He'd been so busy modelling other successful business owners or trying to match the energy of his business partner that everything always felt so fake and weird. To play the new games would require the creation of new personas.

Conclusion

The best way to be human is to be aligned *with* life and work *with* yourself rather than to position yourself *against* life and to fight *against* yourself. Your true essence is the essence of life itself. They are one and the same thing.

The best thing about the self-permission model is that it dramatically speeds up the process of helping you do this very thing!

Sometimes self-awareness can feel like a wide-open field with no perimeters.

> How do I even know what to search for, or if I've found the right thing?

Yet, knowing that there are only ever four conditions to be satisfied to gain or regain permission from yourself, greatly narrows the search field so that you can know for certain what you are looking for and where to find the answer.

In every case it is only a breech in one or more of the four conditions. That means that to regain permission your work is to stay within these four areas until you've solved the problem again.

1. Trust – Reopen the criminal case you've held against yourself to find all historic accusations false. Completely repair the damage caused by the self-betrayal perpetrated by living as though the accusation was true and come to trust your natural ability without having to manage yourself.

2. Notice the catastrophic strategy you've developed off the back of this childhood accusation to cover your fears and meet your needs. Having dissolved the fear, you are now free to redesign the strategy and meet all needs internally instead.

3. Due to your underlying lack of trust in yourself notice how you've inadvertently followed other people's lead into games that are NOT suited to you. Now that trust is restored you are free to listen to your own wisdom about the kind of games you've always desired to play instead. Because you no longer need other people's approval or permission to be safe, go ahead and exit their games and enrol in your games.

4. Notice that each of the games you've been playing have required you to create certain personas to continue playing. Understand that these personas are NOT who you really are but have been strategically created to meet your needs and protect your fears in a very transactional way. Each new game you've enrolled in will require the creation of a new avatar who knows how to win these games.

This exact process works for me, and it will work for you too.

www.ingramcontent.com/pod-product-compliance
Lightning Source LLC
Chambersburg PA
CBHW031244290426
44109CB00012B/423